Community-in-a-Box

How to Build Event-Driven Professional Communities

Mark Birch

Table of Contents

FOREWORD

By Xiaoyin Qi, Founder and CEO of Run The World

Wanting a sense of community is human nature. Yet, very few people know how to build lasting communities. Especially this year, when COVID has broken the world apart and deprived us from having those friendly gatherings, happy hours, meetups, conferences, or even casual dinners, the old way of building communities simply didn't work.

What do we do?

I am glad we have Mark. He is one of the savviest community builders and has built one of the most influential communities, Enterprise Sales Forum, in the world. I met Mark this year, when we just launched Run The World, a virtual events platform enabling people to meet each other online. We were lucky to launch the company the week before COVID hit and saw overwhelming demands, but we struggled to explain why we do what we do.

At Run The World, we did not think the future of events was another webinar, but experiences where attendees could meet each other. Internally, we even used the number of attendees interacting with each other as one of our top line metrics, but that was May 2020, two months after COVID hit, and most people were still trying to figure out how to replicate a physical event online. We had a hard time persuading people why they should use our cocktail party (matching attendees with one another every 5 minutes, like speed dating) instead of another webinar. Or why a virtual event reception desk is not necessary; instead, use an online chat group that can last even after the event finished. When I met Mark, he instantly got it. He was telling us all the experiments he had tried, and why online events should be better measured by the interaction level of attendees, instead of simply getting more attendees. He also started talking about how to better curate the audience, and figured out the right icebreaker for them to get connected. I have seen hundreds of online events, but I immediately realized this was the customer who knew more than I did. Mark has the rare first principles thinking for community building.

Over time, we started to collaborate more with Mark, and I enjoyed showing him what's new and got his feedback. I also observed how devoted and proactive his volunteers were at creating warm and enlightening event experiences, entirely autonomously. Mark has really figured out a scalable, repeatable process to build strong community that can last smoothly, despite big turmoil like the one we are in today.

I loved reading this book. I wish he published it the year before; I just raised my seed round, designing and coding for Run The World (runtheworld.today). I probably would have wasted less time building product features that were proven to be wrong later and made fewer mistakes if he had. I really recommend this book to anyone who wants to build long-lasting communities that connect like-minded people together.

WELCOME

Congratulations, you want to start a community!

The desire for people to gather together has existed since the dawn of humanity. Community is something innate in all of us; being driven to belong and the need to be part of something beyond our own existence. We are bound by the desire to connect and share our interests, hopes, and dreams.

When I started the Enterprise Sales Forum, I did not have a noble purpose or big vision. It was an easy way to get salespeople and startup founders to meet and help each other. Some were from startups I had invested in or advised, while others were simply struggling with the challenges of business-to-business ("B2B") sales and needed advice.

The setup was not novel. I asked a few friends to speak, invited another friend to help out, and then let my network know I was hosting an event at my office. I had a conference room booked that could hold up to 50 people, though I expected 25 to show up; over 80 attended. Since that first event, the group has grown to 25,000 members over 20 cities globally.

Along the way, I learned a lot about what it takes to create a sustainable community. From the perspective of those on the outside, it looks easy. However, nothing could be further from the truth. When I looked around at similar groups, I noticed many died out after three or four events; only a tiny fraction ever made it past one year.

That is not to say that I didn't make plenty of mistakes over the course of hosting over 300 events. There were speakers who were no-shows and disappearing food deliveries. There were ticket foibles and gatecrashers. There were scheduling snafus and last minute venue changes. Through plenty of trial and error, I learned a lot, the hard way.

I firmly believe, however, that building a community is an amazing experience. While we all approach community building with our own motivations, the end result is a labor of love that positively impacts the lives of many. Through the Enterprise Sales Forum, people found jobs, connected with mentors, transacted deals, launched companies, and turned around careers.

That is my hope for you—to positively impact lives through your community while avoiding the many mistakes I made. I have gathered over six years of experience in what it takes to build a community to share with you. This is what I found to work, but you may find other methods that work for you. My suggestion for using this *Community-in-a-Box* is to experiment with the formula inside and see what fits your situation.

I have included my contact information in the index if you have further questions. Feel free to reach out, let me know how you are getting along, but most of all, enjoy the experience. I am sure you will build an amazing community!

Mark Birch
Founder of DEVBIZOPS & Enterprise Sales Forum

INTRODUCTION

This book is a labor of love and a bit of a catharsis. It is a nuts and bolts, how-to book interspersed with the blood and guts of what it took to learn the ropes of community building between the pages. I spent as much time ruminating and reminiscing on the journey as I did writing the content.

The typical way to structure these types of books is to put the story first. Each chapter is some funny vignette or heart-wrenching lesson, all stitched together with some narrative thread. In the process, somehow, a few nuggets of sound advice and practical information get shared along the way.

That is not how I approached this project. In fact, this book is a bit of an accident. It started off as the 18 page operations guide for launching new local chapters of the Enterprise Sales Forum. Then the book sat for a few years before I dusted it off and gave it a fresh batch of updates in an attempt to make it more generic for other communities. The project died though, as other urgent matters pulled me away.

Then someone at my current employer, Amazon Web Services, asked about a "user manual" for launching user groups. That sounded vaguely like a community, so I shared this now 31-page handbook with my manager to pass along in an attempt to be helpful.

Nothing came of sending along my handbook, but it dawned on me that I had not included anything about virtual events. The Enterprise Sales Forum had recently switched to all virtual events, so there was a whole body of knowledge to share that was way more relevant than the sole focus of in-person events.

After a furious week of writing, I finally had over 50 pages and was brimming with confidence that I had my first book in the bag! All that was left was to proofread and clean up the awkward parts. For assistance, I reached out to my network and shared the first full draft with some folks, about twenty people in all.

I would not say the feedback was brutal, as these are all super nice and generous people. The feedback was very candid and direct though. The critiques drove home the fact that the book was a mess. The order of topics made no sense, there were huge assumptions built in, and there were gaps in the content on topics I neglected to include. On top of it, my grammar mistakes were atrocious.

With that information, I went back to the book to rearrange and reorganize everything. Whole chapters were rewritten and I added more content to fill in the gaps. What emerged was a solid 70 pages of content, but there was still a problem. I filled the pages with information about starting a community, but wrote nothing that incorporated what I learned in six years of leading the Enterprise Sales Forum about sustaining and growing communities!

This time, I hit the whiteboard to sketch out what a long-standing community resembles and the path a community takes to get there. My experiences, recollections, and searing memories were laid bare across two whiteboards. It got hard following all the arrows, but I think most of what poured out of my head made it into this book, a now dense 150ish pages of content, tips, and practical how-tos.

Why Publish this Now?

It is probably a good time to point out that I am writing a book about event-driven communities in a year when the entire world of events has been turned upside down. For good reason, all events and conferences globally have either been cancelled or switched to online.

With the world still in a state of disruption and uncertainty, why release this book now? Simply because the desire of people to connect never diminishes. In fact, community matters even more during times of extreme duress and hardship. It has been amazing to see the energy and enthusiasm of people finding ways to bring communities together during a time of social distancing.

The Enterprise Sales Forum had the same challenge as every other community. How do we transfer the experience of in-person events to digital engagement? The team experimented with various formats and platforms to find the right mix of engagement and stability, finally settling on Run The World as the online platform for the community.

At some point, the world will beat back the virus. When that happens, people will once again gather together. There may be an easing-in period for the sake of precaution, but there is no denying the fact that the in-person experience will not disappear. If anything, we have gained valuable expertise in managing virtual experiences, which in turn has enriched and expanded the reach of communities.

Many of the best entrepreneurs and startups emerged stronger from past downturns when the economy started growing again. This was because they looked ahead and prepared for the time when business would pick up. The world is in a constant state of change; with every downturn follows an eventual upturn.

In the same way, now is the best time to think about community, both in the virtual and in-person worlds. I would even be so bold as to declare that 2020 has launched us into the Age of Community. So let's get building!

Who is this Book for?

I wrote this book with three specific audiences in mind. First, I wrote it for people like me, the lone person with an idea for a professional community, but no idea how best to start. Second, there is the community organizer already on the journey, yet looking for ideas to improve, grow, and scale the community they have already launched. Third, with many companies hopping on the community bandwagon, I wrote it for the person within an organization tasked with building a community around customers, users, partners, donors, or constituents.

However, this is a book that can be helpful for anyone who is looking to rally people around a vision. The gathering of people for a common cause is a powerful dynamic, whether in the corporate boardroom, the workplace lunchroom, the classroom, or the ball field in the park. The concepts shared in this book can be easily applied to harnessing the human potential of groups as we have all seen on social networks, open source software development, and crowdsourcing platforms.

What Should you Expect to Find?

There are many great sources for community-oriented information these days. There are websites dedicated to community, blogs posts with great insights, podcasts and videos, active Twitter community folks, as well as various books on the topic. So what makes this book any different?

With *Community-in-a-Box*, I had three goals in mind:

- **Share the real-life experiences from successfully building communities;**
- **Put all those experiences into one, well-organized, easy to follow resource; and**
- **Focus on timeless principles and practical methods of community building.**

Building community is like starting anything—awkward and painful at first. As much as I am a cheerleader for communities, it is also important to be fully transparent about all the obstacles along the way. While it is humbling to expose many of my own mistakes here, I am hopeful you can take the lessons shared and avoid the same missteps.

When I was building the Enterprise Sales Forum, I tried searching for good advice about how to sustain and scale a community. I had some good conversations with people from other meetups and groups, but I got the sense we were all searching for the same thing, and completely in the dark. All we wanted was a guide that could help us find our way through the unknowns of community building.

This led me to write up the operations guide for the Enterprise Sales Forum. I needed a convenient way to convey what I had learned into something that could be useful for any of my chapter leaders when I was not around to answer questions. There is still an operations guide feel to some of the structure and writing; however, unlike other books on community, this one is meant to be a reference guide that you come back to often as you have questions.

The other issue I came across in my research on community building was that a lot of advice was either very shallow or tool-oriented. I kept asking myself how this information was relevant and why there was one certain path versus a different path? The reasoning behind the "why" is important because those principles do not change over time. When you build on that foundation of core principles, the methods and tools are not as important, and can be replaced for better options down the road.

The frustration I experienced with many how-to oriented books is that they rely so heavily on the tools, which can quickly become irrelevant. I remember reading a sales book several years back that included a list of "guaranteed to open email subject lines." A week later I started receiving emails with these subject lines. Within six months, the usefulness of those subject lines was completely erased.

To avoid that same mistake, I focused on the content and not on tools so the usefulness of this book has a longer shelf life. Content on principles and proven methods that stand the test of time make up the bulk of the book. The content more likely to change, such as tools, technologies, and still-evolving concepts is placed in the Appendix as easily referenced questions.

How is the Book Organized?

This book is structured in five parts: The Right Foundation, Building the Community, Sustaining the Community, Parting Thoughts, and the Appendix. The chapters within each part capture core ideas and are deliberately short to assure the usefulness of this guidebook.

- **The Right Foundation** – I discuss foundational considerations of community building you should ponder before you get started on building your community, such as why the community is needed and your motivations for leading the launch of the community. After all my dire warnings, if you still want to proceed, make sure to take the "I, Community Organizer" pledge!

- **Building the Community** – The bulk of the content in this book is in this part, presented as the ten steps needed to launch a self-sustaining and healthy community. The chapters focus on fundamentals that can be broadly applied to any community. Some of the chapters are quite detailed, especially for managing events. The idea is to utilize these as templates for your community's operating procedures.

- **Sustaining the Community** – I shift gears slightly in this part to focus more on broader principles of growing community and thinking for the long-term. I describe the five principles required to build a long-lasting, stable community. I also share some of the common challenges that occur along the way and ask the question of whether it makes sense to scale the community.

- **Parting Thoughts** – I provide some last bits of encouragement and support as you go off on your own community journey. I also thank many of the people responsible for making this book possible.

- **Appendix** – I structured this part as a FAQs with questions that address topics on tools, technologies, and processes. The content will change often given that technology and methods change rapidly, so expect to see updates for this section to be available on the book's website. Additionally, you will find examples of checklists to utilize within your own community.

Most authors will suggest you read from beginning to end. You could do that with this book, but I also think you should feel free to bounce around as you wish when questions or issues arise. While the book is organized to build upon itself, you may be in a different stage in your journey or have more targeted and urgent needs. If a part does not apply to you, skip it and move on. *Community-in-a-Box* in that sense is like those "Choose Your Own Adventure" books, but in this case your adventure is the quest to build an awesome community.

Are there Additional Materials for this Book?

Check out the *Community-in-a-Box* website (www.community-in-a-box.com) to find additional resources and updates to the content in this book and to sign up for the newsletter. In the newsletter, I will share announcements to invite you to join the "Community Coffee Chats" online community and Run The World video talks, which I am hosting to bring together people inspired by and using the content from this book to build awesome communities.

As your community grows, keeping the excitement and enthusiasm going through the ups and downs can leave you drained. We still do it because what drives us to start a community is the desire to change something in the world for the benefit of others through the power of connection. So reach out to the community of community builders, as we are here to help each other!

PART 1 - THE RIGHT FOUNDATION

"Alone, we can do so little; together, we can do so much."

– Helen Keller

THE PERSONAL VALUE OF COMMUNITY

My journey into the world of community started from the ashes of a failing tech startup over a decade ago. I was a co-founder of a company launching an enterprise human resource analytics platform during a time when the world's financial systems were on the brink of collapse.

While the global economy certainly did not help, the problems with my startup were more profound and self-inflicted. I learned three key lessons from that failure:

- Tech startups should not outsource their tech.

- Choose your business partners very carefully.

- Networking with startups, investors, and advisors is not optional.

I could write another book just about the first two lessons alone, but the third lesson speaks directly to the idea of community. Driven by ego and pride, I was exclusively relying upon myself to figure things out, though I was getting a lot wrong and making critical mistakes along the way.

The startup folded, but the lesson about networking hit home. It was 2009, and I jumped headlong into the Meetup culture in New York City (NYC) to start building the network that I lacked during my startup journey. I went on a tech startup meetup binge, going to an event every evening of the weekday, and sometimes even doubling or tripling up.

It was during this time that I met a couple of guys looking to bring in top entrepreneurs across NYC to be part of a new startup accelerator program. It was called WeWork Labs, and being part of that first group of fifty was an incredible experience in seeing how a community takes shape. It was the catalyst for shifting my thinking about the importance of community dynamics in unleashing human potential and value creation.

Building a network and being active in the community led to incredible opportunities. I took the lesson of "give to get," from well-known venture capitalist Brad Feld, to heart, offering my time to entrepreneurs during office hours, advising startup founders, and freely dispensing lessons learned on my blog and growing social media presence. This led to building a great portfolio of startup investments, access to fellow investors and influencers, speaking opportunities, and consulting gigs advising startup founders on building their sales processes and teams.

One minor downside was the challenge of managing my time. I had a habit of saying "yes" to all meetings, so I would often meet with a dozen or so startup founders a day in between my other work. Often, each meeting was about the same topic, how to sell to big businesses.

I loved meeting with entrepreneurs, yet, at the same time, it was incredibly draining. It seemed wasteful to convey the same information over and over again. If all these folks have the same questions, why not bring them together with experts on sales to learn as a group? That was the birth of the Enterprise Sales Forum.

Consequently, in August 2014, I ran an experiment to see if anyone would come. Six years later, the experiment turned into a movement to catalyze sales professionals worldwide to raise the bar on sales skills and acumen. Of all of my professional achievements, the Enterprise Sales Forum will forever be my proudest.

I share this story because community is not just about building value for others. Community will transform you in ways you will not expect, and always for the better. When you get started on the path of building a community, you will be pushed to learn more, to become resilient, to grow emotionally, and to become a leader of people. I learned all those lessons, and then some.

The value you take from the experience depends on you. Keeping an open mind, taking on calculated risks, staying humble, delegating work, and owning mistakes goes a long way in accelerating your learning and your results. I know this from my own experience and have learned more in these past few years than I ever did at any point in my professional life.

Do not be discouraged that the journey is hard at first! I messed up more times than I care to admit. I alienated chapter leaders, goofed up event logistics, said many dumb things, pissed off sponsors, and got into needless spats with members. That is why I am sharing this book with you, so you can avoid the pitfalls towards building a healthy community.

WHAT IS YOUR COMMUNITY?

The textbook definition of community is "a group of people with a common characteristic or interest living together within a larger society."[1] Another useful explanation for defining a community that I often relied upon is:

A group of people with a common interest and shared values.

Given these definitions, what makes your community distinct? What is that common thread that brings people together? Once you bring people together, how do you ensure the community remains healthy and grows? To figure out your community, you need to answer four simple questions: what, who, why, and how?

Normally, you would think to start with "why." After all, that is what well-known speakers like Simon Sinek talk about.[2] In general, this is true, which I will share the importance of why later on. In my experience though, most communities start with a mini-"why" seeking a "what."

Community organizers often begin their journey thinking, "I wish there was a group that did 'this thing' I am interested in." There is always some reason, or spark, that gets the idea going. It may not eventually be the big "why" that helps launch the community, but it is enough of a question or pain in the neck that it nudges the process along to finding the "what."

I mentioned the start of the Enterprise Sales Forum was a way to get salespeople and founders together. The spark though for me was way too

---

[1]   Merriam Webster, "Community"; https://www.merriam-webster.com/dictionary/community

[2]   Simon Sinek, "How Great Leaders Inspire Action"
       https://www.ted.com/talks/simon_sinek_how_great_leaders_inspire_action

many coffee meetings explaining the basics of sales to startup founders and mentoring salespeople on enterprise selling. Beside the caffeine headaches, I became frustrated with the lack of reliable information about B2B sales.

Once the spark ignites, the mini-"why" turns into a "what." Would-be community organizers search around online for something, ask friends doing 'this thing' if they know of any groups, and then explore various groups, meetups, and forums to see if any of these meet their expectations.

When I started the Enterprise Sales Forum, the "what" was pretty clear. I was searching for a community of people interested in B2B complex sales so people could learn from each other. Before I decided to start my own community, I searched and asked about groups, but nothing really hit the mark. The events seemed more networking-oriented rather than built about quality content. There were also many non-salespeople in attendance. The experiences from these events helped forge what the Enterprise Sales Forum would become, a community distinct from what already existed.

Your community can be centered around a similar interest, a profession, a company or school, or a lifestyle. It can be anything you want. The point is your community focuses on that one thing and "owns the niche." Once you deviate, you begin to lose what it is that makes your community special, exclusive, and worthwhile to join.

The next important element is "who" is in your community. You can make your community wide open or very exclusive. You can let anyone sign up or implement an application process to evaluate potential members. The core of any community is the people in it, so having the right chemistry is critical. People joining your group should expect they are going to meet and engage with their peers around "what" your community represents.

The Enterprise Sales Forum has an open enrollment in which the community accepts anyone involved in B2B sales or seeking to learn more about B2B sales. The group is still a well-defined niche; selling to businesses tends to be more complex and distinctive enough to catch the attention of the core audience. They feel the community is about them and not the broader profession of sales, which members confirmed in surveys to be an important consideration in joining the community. The "Curating

Membership" chapter discusses refining "who" is in your community.

When you start talking about your community idea with others, you quickly find yourself answering the "why" question. Mostly, people will want to know "why" others should join. Just responding with, "There is no community for 'this thing' and people will love it," is not a strong basis to begin, so it is worth taking the time to describe the "why" of the community.

There are two key questions to ask yourself:

- **Why do you think your community is needed?**
- **What impact will your community make?**

As I started to talk about this B2B sales community I wanted to form, I took the experiences from attending other groups and events to refine what was unique and valuable about the community I wanted to create. There were four things that stood out to me that I wanted to do differently:

- The community should be independent, non-vendor aligned, and about members first;
- The content should be practical, insightful, relevant, and high-quality;
- The people in the group should be open to collaborating and sharing; and
- The community should be open to innovative approaches in selling.

I took these thoughts and molded them into the "why" for the Enterprise Sales Forum. The community now describes itself as a community for B2B salespeople by B2B salespeople to network with peers, to learn from experienced sales professionals, and to collaborate with each other.

The other side of why can almost be thought of as a "so what" question, as in "So what is the impact?" By itself, the Enterprise Sales Forum's "why" makes sense. But why does this community really matter and what impact will it have on others?

This is where vision comes in. What is vision? Vision is a simple statement that inspires change brought about by the work of an organization. It explains the impact you seek to make in the world. This is the end state and the audacious goal that inspires your community to instigate meaningful change.

The vision for the Enterprise Sales Forum grew from the perception that sales was not a well-respected profession. Training was often rudimentary and outdated. Strategy was little more than "ground and pound" tactics. I felt there were enough like-minded sales professionals that also aspired to something better and wanted to create a community to change the current state of sales. I saw that a community could elevate sales as a noble profession and help sales professionals to grow professionally in their career.

Getting your "why" clearly defined will take a few iterations. Share your "why" with others who will be part of your community and be open to suggestions and changes. You know you have hit upon your "why" when they enthusiastically respond with, "That makes sense," and hopefully ask to sign up!

Which leads us to the question of "how." The bulk of this book dives into how to build an event-driven, professional community. "Event-driven" means members primarily meet and interact in the context of in-person or virtual events. "Professional" means people in a particular job, industry, or trade.

The "how" also touches on the place where your community mostly lives. This is especially important for a world in which virtual events are becoming more commonplace. Communities, now more than ever, are relying on social media sites, discussion forums and messaging groups, and online event platforms to be the gathering places for the community to meet.

It is also important to clarify what the "how" does not cover. This book does not delve specifically into fully online communities or those oriented towards hobbies, social activities, or general interests. Those are topics hefty enough for their own books, but there are still many useful universal lessons shared in this book that can be valuable for communities of all types.

What is your community then? It starts with that spark leading to a "what" that defines your unique niche in the world. By defining "who" the community is for, it draws in people who will gain the most value from your community. Once you know "who," you have to give them a "why" that both explains the purpose of the community and inspires people to want to participate in your community. Lastly, you need to know the "how" your community comes together and do all the awesome things you hope your community achieves!

CAN I DO THIS?

Before I get too far ahead and talk about "how" to run a community, there are two important questions you need to ask yourself:

- **Can I do this?**
- **Am I ready?**

You may wonder whether this is something you are cut out for or if you have the right credentials. Rest assured, the process of starting and leading a community is actually quite achievable, and something I will explain as I discuss how to launch and maintain your community. Luckily, community building does not require any specific training or skills, you can gain those skills as you progress towards establishing your community.

Speaking from experience, I did not think I had any skills in managing a community in the beginning. For the first six months of the Enterprise Sales Forum, I simply thought of it as a meetup where I was running events. What I discovered, though, was how the skills I picked up from doing other things, such as sales and being an entrepreneur, helped me manage the community. I kept an open mind and along the way developed other skills that gave me more confidence to become a capable community manager.

So skills are not as big of a consideration when it comes to community building. We all have the ability and talents that help us on that journey. What does matter is whether you have the *passion* and the *availability* to start a community.

Passion can be thought of as directed motivation. You should be motivated to want to commit to the success of the community over the long-term. Motivation gets to the core reason of "why" you want to start a community. Some useful questions to ask yourself would be:

- What is your motivation to start a community?
- Why are you the right person to start a community?

Take a piece of paper or go to a whiteboard and write down the answers to those two questions. Do not edit yourself. Tap into your stream of consciousness and just write. The answers will help you gauge whether starting a community is for you.

Broadly speaking, when you consider what you have written down, where on the spectrum do your answers fall when you consider your source of motivation and ability to commit time?

- **Selfless vs. Self-Interested**
- **Have Time vs. Time Constrained**

The motivation that unites most community builders is the desire to help others. They consider it an opportunity to do something out of goodwill and to "give back." They are "other-oriented." If your responses to the motivation questions tend to be more self-oriented, then you may want to reconsider whether community building is for you. Some self-interest is to be expected, but when it is the primary driver, it will be hard to muster the energy and willpower when the inevitable challenges and snags occur. Your motivation needs to be greater than yourself.

The other consideration is having the availability to lead a community. You have to be honest when assessing if you have the time and stamina to run a community. You may be starting a family, have an intense work schedule, experience unpredictable travel schedules, or have other existing commitments that would make it difficult to attend to the affairs of the community and run events. Consistency matters when launching and maintaining a community.

I saw both passion and availability play a factor when bringing on chapter leaders for the Enterprise Sales Forum. Some leaders used the community to promote their own businesses; other leaders had the right motivations, but were simply too busy traveling or leading sales teams to dedicate time to the community.

Therefore, passion and availability are the two most important considerations. There are additional traits though that I have found to make for a competent community leader:

- **Understanding of the community** – While it seems obvious, you should have a direct connection to and knowledge of the people with whom you are looking to form a community.

- **Existing network of relevant contacts** – Related to involvement, if you are involved with the people you are looking to organize, you should have a large and well-established network of contacts.

- **Innate desire to help others** – I touched on this before regarding motivation and cannot stress enough the importance of having the "heart" to help others.

- **Strong bias for action** – This simply means you tend to stay on task and get things done, the type of folks I would call "doers" because they roll up their sleeves to do the work.

- **High energy and self-motivated** – Leaders experience plenty of highs and lows, so being resilient to forge ahead and having the internal drive to stay focused on the vision is critical.

- **Embraces a growth mindset** – There will be plenty of new experiences, so the desire to enjoy tackling challenges and learning will make the experience for you more rewarding.

One final thought is that you do not have to already be a leader or notable person to begin. Anyone can be successful in community building! What is more important is having the right characteristics because there will be plenty of challenges and obstacles ahead. That will be the foundation for you to grow into your role as a community organizer and find success.

WILL THEY COME?

One of the worst mistakes you could make early on is assuming that if you build it, they will come. By they, I mean the people you propose to invite and draw into your nascent community. Just because a community scratches your itch, does not mean it will scratch an itch for enough other people to build a thriving community.

Of course, you can never be 100% certain that people will come. That will only be proven over the course of time. For the Enterprise Sales Forum, it was obvious from the first event that it had the potential to be a successful community. Over the course of several months, the community grew quickly. More people outside of my network had heard of the Enterprise Sales Forum, and companies were reaching out to partner or sponsor the community.

In a world with many options and distractions, getting people to notice and take interest in your community is imperative. How to go about doing so will be addressed in a later chapter; however, the paramount question to ask is why would anyone care about your community? Specifically, what is in it for them that would motivate them to join?

Let's talk about motivation for a moment. Previously, I encouraged you to think about why you want to start a community. This helps to establish the vision in your mind, but often that vision can sound aloof to others. You are talking about changing the world, and most people are stuck on what to eat for lunch. The vision needs to connect with everyday practical needs or help solve some obvious challenge in order to be meaningful.

Let's take the Enterprise Sales Forum as an example. Below are some ideas that helped make the vision and value of the community relatable to more explicit needs:

- **Networking** - Salespeople are always looking to build professional relationships that can lead to business opportunities down the road.

- **Learning** - Inviting experienced sales professionals to discuss their tips and tricks for sales success can help fill in knowledge gaps for salespeople looking to improve their results.

- **Sharing Ideas** - Talking to peers introduces ideas and new ways to approach sales strategies and tactics in a friendly, low-stress environment that helps sharpen sales skills.

- **Jobs** - A big motivator for salespeople is to find future opportunities, which is easier to do in the context of a community where salespeople can meet with potential hiring managers.

- **Recruiting** - The flipside of job seeking is candidate seeking, and a community is the perfect place to meet many salespeople and managers to later speak with when opportunities arise.

- **Mentorship** - More junior salespeople learn faster when they can speak with mentors, and seasoned salespeople want to pay it forward to help junior salespeople.

- **Research** - Founders of sales technology startups are always looking for places to meet and interview potential users about innovative solutions and tools they are marketing.

These are only some motivations originally drafted early on for the Enterprise Sales Forum. Consider what those motivations would be to prospective members of the community you are building. Rank them in the order you think are most important.

The next step is to test your theory on motivations with the very people you would want to be in your community. Do not just ask your friends since they are already going to be predisposed to saying nice things and agreeing with everything you say. Seek out people you do not know quite well or even strangers to gauge their opinion, as they will be more likely to give their candid, unvarnished opinions.

The best way to do this discovery work is to set up face-to-face meetings or video calls. I prefer seeing the person because then you can pick up on non-verbal cues. Even if you are stuck with a plain old phone call, the best way to start are with simple, open-ended questions about the community you wish to start and why you wish to start it. Then keep quiet, actively listen, and take notes. Towards the end of the interview time, you can introduce the motivations you came up with and have the interviewee rank those motivations in importance to him or her.

Target ten to fifteen of these short interviews. That is often good enough to get a sense of what is going to be important for the community. Never assume those motivations are static though. As the community grows and adds new members, the types of things that motivate people to come to events and join the community may shift or new motivations may arise.

Be willing to challenge your own assumptions about what you think is important. Community is not about what you want; rather, it is about what the members of the community want. Therefore, take time to survey and interview members of the community to gauge their interests and motivations. This is one way to continually keep the content, experiences, and services of the community fresh, which is discussed in more depth in the "Reinvent and Re-energize" chapter.

I, COMMUNITY ORGANIZER

Recognize that when you make the commitment to create a community, you are the one leading the charge. There is much more to organizing than the activities involved in setting up the group, creating events, and doing the work of community building. First and foremost, you have to be a leader.

Say this out loud,

"I AM A COMMUNITY ORGANIZER!"

Did you yell it out? Did you have enthusiasm? Did you pump your fists into the air and feel the rush of excitement overwhelm you?

Maybe not, and that is okay. Fundamentally though, you need to recognize and embrace this new facet of your life. When you start a community, you are the community organizer. You can get others to help, you can deflect attention away from yourself, but ultimately you are the one leading the charge.

Maybe you do not think of yourself as a leader. If you are reading this, however, you are absolutely a leader. What is a leader? I like what Bill Bradley, former US Senator and National Basketball League star, had to say:

"Leadership is unlocking people's potential to become better."

When you create a community, you create an environment that allows people to become better in some tangible way. The very act of starting a community means you are leading by helping to unlock the potential in others!

So embrace this new facet of your life and let others know that you are a community organizer. When you take charge of this reality, you are on the path towards boldly launching a new community and making a positive impact in this world and the lives of others.

Now, let's get into the guts of how to build a community!

PART 2 - BUILDING THE COMMUNITY

"You don't have to be great to start, but you have to start to be great."

– Zig Ziglar

HOW TO GET STARTED

The process for launching a community can feel daunting in the beginning! If you are systematic and have a process to follow though, things will be much more manageable. Luckily, that is exactly what this entire part is about!

Through my experience in running the Enterprise Sales Forum, I have found ways through trial and many errors to ease the process of getting started and reduce the challenges that always plague the launch of communities. Be that as it may, it is important to stress:

There are no shortcuts in building a great community.

It will take a long time to develop, the numbers of attendees will look small initially, and many setbacks will occur. Community building, like starting a company or building a new sales territory, requires both patience and consistent execution to plan. However, if you follow the plan and remain committed, you will have a thriving community. You just have to have the patience to see it through the early stages.

To launch a community, the following ten things need to be organized:

1) **Establish core values**
2) **Build the founding team**
3) **Venue to host events**
4) **Monetization to cover costs**
5) **Speakers to talk at events**
6) **Content calendar and events schedule**
7) **Promotion to relevant audience**
8) **Curating membership**

9) **Sponsors to support community**

10) **Managing the events**

You may look at this list and immediately feel overwhelmed. You might not think you have what it takes to be a community organizer after your bold declaration. It is common to feel this way early on and to presume you are all alone.

This is why I mention in the previous chapter that having an existing network of relevant contacts is strongly encouraged. You will need to reach out to your network to pull together all aspects of the community and to find companies and people that can help.

Given the importance of your network in the launch stage of your community, I recommend, as a prerequisite, to create a Launch Organizing List. This is a list of people in your network who can help in some aspect of the community. Sometimes, a connection can be helpful in a pinch, such as promoting an upcoming event via social media or making an introduction to a speaker. Every bit of help and sharing is a valuable contribution.

You should begin list building by using LinkedIn to search for first degree connections in your area that are relevant to the community you wish to form. Other people to include might be startup founders, company executives, and employees of notable local companies that can provide space, speakers, and possible sponsorship. You may also want to search through your email and other social media contacts to expand your list, since you may not be connected to everyone you know on LinkedIn.

What if LinkedIn is not heavily used in your country or in the industry you focus on? Go where the people in your community would most likely gather or visit online. There could be Facebook groups, Twitter lists, industry specific sites like GitHub or Dribbble, and any number of sources to find people that most fit your community. While the rest of this book will use LinkedIn as the basis for my examples, modify and apply the tactics used here for your situation. You can also refer to the Appendix for more specific details on building your Launch Organizing List.

Another consideration before getting started on building a community is naming the community. One of the struggles many community founders have in the beginning is coming up with a name that is both catchy and descriptive. It is easy to overthink this decision and put too much emphasis on finding the "right" name early on before the community has even started.

There are two things to keep in mind. First, you are better off using a simple and obvious name rather than something more creative. When I named the Enterprise Sales Meetup (the original name), you might think it is plain, but it clearly captures what the community is about; salespeople who gather at meetups focused on content about selling into large organizations. Second, your prospective members do not care what you call the community (as long as your name is not dumb, offensive, or obscure). They come because they care about the network, content, and vision.

It should also be mentioned that you are not stuck with the name you pick. Changing the name down the road can be a pain for a whole host of reasons, but it can be done. You just need to consider the reasons and the timing for such a decision.

When the community decided to change the name of the Enterprise Sales Meetup to Enterprise Sales Forum three years into the group's existence, it meant changing the website, social media handles, content, email, etc. Even though only one word was being swapped, the community was growing beyond just "meetups" and was also moving off of Meetup.com as a community and events management platform. Removing "Meetup" from the name, therefore, made sense and communicated to members the growth and maturity of the community.

So keep the name of your community simple and straightforward. If you start a community for product managers, then call it the Product Managers Forum or the Product Leaders Collective. Make it clear that your community is for a specific group of people and you will avoid having to heavily curate your community because people joined who did not fit in that specific group.

Once you have built your Launch Organizing List and given your community a name, you have the pieces in place to confidently start the community building journey. Let's dig into each step of the community launch process in more detail.

COMMUNITY VALUES

It is one thing to know why you want to start a community, but do you know what your community stands for? This is distinct from why your community exists, what the community is about, and who the community is for, as previously discussed. You are trying to answer what values your community abides by and how is that demonstrated through the activities of your community.

Values act as a filter for the things you allow and do not allow in your community. It's the glue that ties the "why", "what", and "who" together and gives it meaningful shape. As a community organizer, it allows you to prioritize what is important and exclude things that would be a distraction. Likewise, observers from the outside can understand more clearly what your community actually stands for, or represents.

This is what is meant by shared values in the definition of community. Values help define a community from a group of people that happen to do the same thing or have a similar interest. By having a stated and agreed upon set of values, the community becomes unique and that uniqueness creates a culture.

Establishing values for the Enterprise Sales Forum early on helped foster a culture of openness, learning, and helping each other. The vision from the very beginning was to create a member-centric community that offered great content and a supportive environment for the purpose of spreading sales innovation. This meant focusing on education, volunteer-driven initiatives, and encouraging people to help each other. Conversely, vendor-oriented product content, heavy reliance on sponsors, and people actively promoting themselves were actively discouraged.

Over time, the values of the Enterprise Sales Forum were refined to four core tenets:

- **Being Member-Centric**
- **Excellence in Content**
- **Supportive and Collaborative**
- **Foster Sales Innovation**

These values have helped define the community and have come to represent how members of the community perceive the Enterprise Sales Forum. Often times, members have mentioned how open and welcoming people are during events and how they always take away some useful information from the content. This is a perfect example of how values set the perception.

Write down what values you espouse. Be clear on that from the outset so there is no confusion about the initiatives you will support, organizations you partner with, and people you allow to join the community. If you find your values shift over time, be sure to understand the impact on the community and to see if you need to course correct or go full steam ahead. Your values will be your compass, so make sure you are heading in the right direction.

BUILDING A TEAM

While you may have the energy and enthusiasm to launch your community, you will quickly find that going it alone will drive you to exhaustion. From my analysis of what makes for successful communities, the number one determinate was the quality of the founding team that launched the community.

Building a healthy community requires a team. Who is a good candidate to join the team? Two things should standout when answering this question: (1) they love what you do; and (2) they have a passion for the vision of the community. Without that passion, they will not last long, especially when challenges arise.

Once passion is established, there are four useful traits to look for. First, they need to have the heart to help others. Second, they should be involved in the profession or endeavor that you are building a community around. Third, they should have a growth mindset. This trait is often overlooked but is critical because building a community from the ground up requires the willingness to learn, experiment, fail, and iterate quickly. You want people that thrive in a changing and dynamic environment. Fourth, they can make time and will make and accommodate their schedule to support the community.

While identifying good team members is not cut and dry, unsuitable ones are very obvious. People that are arrogant, flakey, egotistical, self-centered, argumentative, dishonest, unmotivated, and jerks do not conform to the ethos of community building and helping others. You want doers who are humble, willing to roll up their sleeves, and work well with others to get stuff done.

It is important to recognize that self-interest is a valid part of the motivation to get involved. There is an altruistic side of wanting to help others. There is also the desire to raise your professional profile, build your network, and create future opportunities. Those are all worthwhile and rational reasons to want to join a community. Therefore, have a candid conversation with each person you ask to join your team about their reasons for wanting to get involved. It is important to be transparent about motivations and not let those personal interests supersede what is best for the community.

How do you find those committed and passionate people to join the founding team? You might be fortunate to launch the community with people you already know, or because the idea emerged from conversations with a few other like-minded people who decided to form a team. If not, this is where having a strong network helps. Use the Launch Organizing List discussed earlier to identify potential team members. I also recommend you expand your outreach by announcing on social networks, like LinkedIn, Facebook, and others, your intentions to launch a community and ask your network to share with others. Take note of people who engage your posts and add them to the pool of people to invite on the initial team call. Those that show up are your potential founding team members.

What is the ideal team size at the start? Anywhere from three to five people is best. It is not too big to make coordination an issue, yet is enough to fairly balance the work. On that first call, discuss the vision and values of the community, the steps to launch the community, and the key roles to fill. While there are many ways to delegate tasks, the following roles work best for the Enterprise Sales Forum:

- **Chapter Leader**: This is the person who makes the final call on key decisions and is often considered the visionary and inspirational leader of the community.
- **Head of Content**: This role is responsible for the content calendar, recruiting speakers, setting the event format, and preparing speakers for upcoming events.
- **Head of Events**: This person is highly detail-oriented and coordinates event needs with venues, as well as managing all aspects of the event experience.

- ☐ **Head of Promotion:** This role organizes all efforts to spread awareness of community, manages communications, promotes events, and drives membership growth.
- ☐ **Head of Sponsorships:** This person secures host sponsors and other local sponsors to ensure the financial health of the community.

This does not mean the above roles would be the best structure for your community. Some communities may want a Head of Membership, for example, to address member experience and data. The point of assigning designated roles is to ensure each member of the founding team takes ownership of some aspect of launching and managing the community. Mix roles together if you like or create new roles, it is up to you.

The number one question that will be asked by potential team members is the time commitment. Each community will be different in this regard, but often community founders on average spend anywhere from 10 to 20 hours per week initially on launching and supporting the community. The good news is that over time, this level of commitment will drop off considerably as more team members join, volunteers are added, and processes are established to automate, outsource, and ease the amount of work needed.

When the community has found a good rhythm after launching, the time commitment tends to be 5 to 10 hours per week on average. Time commitment will vary between roles as well. For example, the key events person is busiest the week before and during the event whereas the person running content is busier several weeks prior to recruit speakers.

Once you have outlined the general roles and responsibilities, give people on the initial call a few days to think on how they would like to be involved. Those who reach out to claim a role will be part of your founding team. If you have multiple people claim a role, make them co-heads of that role. If you have other people that wish to be involved with a lower level of commitment, make them a volunteer (see the "Recruiting Volunteers" chapter).

Over time, it will become obvious who is truly committed to the community. You can see it in the work they produce and energy they exude. As mentioned, community building is a long journey, so expect to see lots of turnover in the leadership ranks. However, if the vision and values remain consistent and the content is strong, there will be others who will raise their hands to become volunteers and leaders.

FINDING A VENUE

The next step in building your community is identifying spaces to host events. Before 2020, this would most certainly have meant a physical space for an in-person gathering. In a world of social distancing, regular mask-wearing, and limited gathering sizes, in-person events have shifted exclusively to virtual experiences, mostly in the format of a webinar.

The post-2020 future will most definitely be one in which in-person and virtual experiences are mixed in a new era of digital events. Given the recent experience built up in delivering events of all sizes in virtual mediums, the economical, logistical, and societal benefits of virtual experiences will ensure that most events will have a virtual component. In fact, a number of large conferences have even indicated they will continue on as virtual only events.

In-person events, however, are here to stay. While technology for hosting virtual events and digital community building has improved rapidly, there is nothing that can replace the experience of bringing humans together. We are a social species and crave experiences that bring like-minded people together in close proximity. The face-to-face experience is one of intimacy and engagement with numerous studies confirming the power of connecting in person.

Does that mean you have to do both? Absolutely not, especially when you are just launching your community. The best strategy is to start simple and build your community in one medium first and then migrate to a multi-medium experience as your community grows. Whether you choose to first focus on in-person or virtual experiences will also heavily depend on prevailing regulations and sensitivities pertaining to in-person gatherings.

Virtual Venue Considerations

Probably the biggest advantage to virtual events is that your venue is literally in the cloud. All of the work required to secure a physical space is off the table, meaning you can give much more attention and time to finding speakers, creating content, and promoting the event. This will be a huge relief to many community organizers since securing venues is almost always the most time-consuming task.

The main consideration when creating a virtual event is finding the appropriate software that facilitates content delivery and interactivity. The number of options has exploded over the years and will continue to expand as more and more communities shift to online events. It is important to understand what to optimize for when thinking about crafting a virtual experience.

- **Platform** – How does the software hosting your event operate?
- **Participation** – How do speakers, organizers, volunteers, and attendees engage?
- **Interactivity** – What level of engagement do you expect?
- **Delivery** – Are the speakers live or pre-recorded?
- **Audience Size** – How many people will participate?
- **Session** – Is it a single, continuous event, or one with multiple tracks?
- **Accessibility** – Does the platform support members with disabilities?
- **Bandwidth** – How much bandwidth will the platform require?
- **Audio / Visual** – Do all speakers and active participants have good quality equipment?
- **Support** – Does the platform have real-time support for issues?
- **Regionalization** – Will the event be open to a local, regional, or global audience?
- **Cost** – Does the platform have a usable free tier, or will it require a paid account?

The virtual setting poses several unique challenges that tend to be less problematic for in-person events. First, capturing the attention of attendees and maintaining their focus on your event requires greater creativity. In-person events benefit from social pressure that ensure attendees are engaged, something that does not exist in a digital space. Second, you have less control over audio / visual quality since you cannot control issues such as equipment used by speakers and attendees or the strength of bandwidth when connecting to the event. Third, the platform itself can be unstable and create a sub-optimal attendee and speaker experience. I discuss platforms in more depth in the Appendix given how rapidly technology changes, but in my experience, even the most well-known and "proven" platforms can experience failures, security issues, and outages unexpectedly.

Creating a positive virtual experience means paying close attention to balancing reach and interactivity with reliability and quality. Even though you may want 500 people on a regional scale, perhaps it makes sense to have a smaller number to avoid bandwidth issues. You could set up a multi-track program with many sessions, but maybe a single-track, single session program is more straightforward for your audience to follow and poses less logistical confusion for organizers and volunteers.

The benefit of a virtual environment is that you can have the same "venue" for all your events. This allows you to test the platform rigorously (and I highly recommend testing often) and iterate quickly on new ideas and changes to formats. You can also run many more events because you are no longer limited by physical space limitations; you can provide the flexibility to try many different formats, expand the content offerings, and bring on many more speakers. The biggest factors limiting your flexibility and scale will be volunteers to help and the cost (discussed later).

The Enterprise Sales Forum has led virtual sessions using different platforms and formats. In some cases, events have been held in a more fireside chat / interview style with actively monitored Q&A throughout. In other instances, the team organized a formal panel with breakout rooms and even a speed networking session. Because physical space is no longer a consideration, you have much more latitude and creativity in how you organize events!

In-Person Venue Considerations

While virtual events have no physical limits and thus more flexible, physical space is a very real consideration with in-person events. That being said, there are still plenty of suitable venue options for in-person events, depending on the size and style of the event. Think of all the large companies, office parks, co-working spaces, startup / business accelerators, business services firms (law firms, banks, consultants, etc.), municipal buildings like libraries, universities, and conference centers, in your area. The biggest challenge is not in booking those venues, but in securing those spaces for free.

A quick word about "free." I am a firm believer in fairly compensating people and organizations for their resources. On the other hand, starting a community from scratch is a daunting task and the prospect of having to fund events out of your own pocket or to find sponsors before you have even begun is enough to stop any momentum. You need to get comfortable with asking for free resources. Sponsorships will be examined in more depth later, but for now consider your first sponsor the venue you are choosing for hosting events.

Why would any organization be willing to offer their space for free? There is a definite cost that the organization incurs, from the extra work by staff to catering and facility fees. Plus, there is the risk and liability of hosting anywhere from a few dozen to well over one hundred outsiders in their offices.

There are plenty of companies that actively seek and desire relevant communities to host events in their facilities. Motivations can range from recruiting to business development to brand exposure. The most common motivation for companies to host a community is urgent hiring needs. When researching venues to host, search for companies that often host events (check sites like Eventbrite and Meetup.com), are rapidly hiring or going to hire because of additional funding, or recently moved into newer, larger offices. Another way to find potential hosts is to search for companies with cool and hip office spaces, as these companies want to showcase their offices and provide the public a positive impression of their facilities and culture.

Given the above thoughts on companies willing to support free events, startups, accelerator programs, and co-working spaces are generally the best options. WeWork and Industrious are just two examples of co-working locations that have hosted the Enterprise Sales Forum. Startups are also good options for hosting and many growth stage startups have open office designs and large common areas conducive for hosting small to mid-sized groups.

Sometimes larger companies may be willing to open up their doors to outside communities. Some even actively court groups to host events in their facilities. The advantage is larger companies generally have the space plus the resources to host outside events. The downside is often such venues will require your group to sign legal agreements that could make you personally liable if anything bad should occur during the course of the event. Avoid such agreements in the early stages of building your community. Even if the company does not push legal requirements, be on the lookout for waivers they may require attendees to sign or onerous security procedures that can impact the guest experience.

Once you have identified a handful of potential venue options, it is time to reach out. The best way to start the conversation on hosting is with an employee with seniority who has an obvious interest in the content of your community and has the authority to make decisions. The Enterprise Sales Forum reaches out to a VP of Sales or Recruiting, as both positions have a keen interest in hiring. The key is to convey the vision of your community and the benefits it can provide to the executive and the company. On the other hand, avoid starting with office managers, low-level recruiters, or facilities people. You need to work with people who have a passion to help your community thrive and are motivated to help.

To find the right people to reach out to, use tools like LinkedIn. When you find the appropriate people, you can send a short InMail or connection request. Below is a sample from the Enterprise Sales Forum:

Hello [First_Name],

I saw your impressive background in [Industry] and wanted to connect. I am the founder of the [Local_Chapter] Enterprise Sales Forum, a community for sales pros to share, network & learn. We seek a venue for our [Date] event and wanted to ask if [Company] would be open to hosting. I look forward to chatting this week. Thanks!

[Your_Name]

The shorter and more direct the message, the more likely you will receive a response. Note that you may need to send multiple messages and also contact multiple people in the company before you get a response. If LinkedIn or email or other social channels do not succeed, then try to find a referral into the company from someone who is willing to help you.

There are other venue options for hosting events. Since the focus is on free, it would be best to avoid certain categories of venues such as conference centers and hotels. While such venues have quality meeting facilities and the experience to host events of varying sizes, they do not offer anything for free. Everything from AV to Wi-Fi to catering comes with significant markups, further inflating your costs beyond just the cost of booking the room.

Even if a company or organization is willing to host, not all venues are created equal. Some are great and others can be a challenge. You need to consider the following when determining an ideal venue:

- **Population** – Is the venue located in the main business district where your members work?

- **Accessibility** – Does the venue accommodate members with disabilities?

- **Travel** – Is it easily accessible via public transportation? Are parking facilities nearby?

- **Space** – Is there adequate space with seating large enough for your group?

- **Availability** – Can they host an event during the hours your community meets?

- **Experience** – Have they hosted previous events and understand the expectations of hosting?

- **Equipment** – Do they have a proper AV setup (mics, PA, projector, etc.)?

- ☐ **Catering** – Do they allow serving of outside food and alcoholic beverages?

- ☐ **Facilities** – Are bathrooms, HVAC, lightning, etc., readily accessible?

- ☐ **Ease** – Are the venue staff easy to work with and open to helping?

- ☐ **Staff** – Do they have people to help handle setup and cleanup for the events?

Another point is the openness of a venue host to cover food and beverage costs. Having food and beverage available is an important aspect of the community experience, particularly during networking time. In many cases, venue sponsors are willing to provide food and beverage, which takes care of those costs and logistics when managing the events. This is not a time to be shy; make sure you are explicit when asking venue hosts on their willingness to provide food and beverages for the events.

Room layout is another critical aspect of hosting events. Big, open areas are preferable over conference room or auditorium style settings. An open area provides the room for networking and you have flexibility of arranging the seats based on attendance and the format of the event.

I am often asked whether restaurants, clubs, entertainment establishments, or bars could be viable venues for events. I have found professional business settings are a better venue for the Enterprise Sales Forum. You may find a more casual environment works better for your group or offers a convenient change of pace.

The convenience of restaurants and the like is that they are setup for events. They have experience hosting events, including private rooms, and have catering services. Even if the room is free, however, added services like AV setup, Wi-Fi, and catering are not covered and can quickly escalate. If you are booking such establishments, be certain that costs are spelled out clearly well before the event starts.

One additional option to consider is hosting at your own company. Often this is the easiest and quickest option if your company has the available space and meets the criteria established above. The advantage is that it eases the logistics of hosting events and you have coworkers who you can ask to volunteer for the day of the event.

When you do finally secure an acceptable venue, can you continue to use it in the future? While having a space for your first event is great, have you considered where the next six events will be held? The benefit of having a "home" for your community is obvious. You have the convenience of reliability, the familiarity of running events in the venue, and it's easier for your members to find. Therefore, ask what the on-going availability is for the space and lock in event dates as far in advance as possible.

At the same time, be flexible in the early days of your community to experiment and find a "home" that fits the nature and purpose of the community. You may find that more social settings like bars and restaurants are a better fit, or that you find an auditorium more appropriate if your group is specifically education-focused. Your goal is to find the very best venue for your community. When you do find the right venue, you will feel it in the energy of the community members during events.

Mixed Venue Considerations

Can you do both in-person and virtual gatherings? Of course! If you decide to go this route though, make sure the virtual experience is not so watered down from the in-person experience that online attendees feel like second-class citizens. Your members and audience deserve a quality experience regardless of channel, plus this will benefit you as an organizer many times over down the road.

When I started the Enterprise Sales Forum, I often received feedback that members loved the idea of the community, but could not often attend events due to work. To serve those members, the Enterprise Sales Forum created a Livestream account to allow members to view the event from wherever they were and still get value from the content being created. The one disadvantage was not having enough volunteers to monitor the Livestream to make it an interactive experience.

Giving equal attention is the core challenge with mixing the in-person and virtual experience. Therefore, it often makes sense to have one person on the team dedicated to monitoring and interacting online during the event to address questions that come up, manage speaker Q&A, and engage attendees both during and in-between sessions.

Note that you may be tempted to charge admissions for the in-person event and allow online viewing for free. This was exactly the model I employed for the Enterprise Sales Forum. In hindsight though, this approach is not recommended since your audience should deserve equal treatment and access no matter which channel they wish to use. Furthermore, by making the online experience free, you are implicitly signaling that online events are of lesser value, undermining the ability to charge for online only events in the future.

Treat all in-person and virtual experiences as equals. This will create less issues later on and convey that what matters most is the content, not the channel by which members access the content.

MONETIZATION

Earlier, I touched on the topic of costs. Regardless of in-person, virtual, or mixed-venue options, you will run into costs for using an online platform or hosting an in-person event. The topic of monetization, therefore, is an important one to spend some time considering.

For virtual events, the software platform you use might not be free. Most SaaS software does have a free tier that can sometimes be useful to start, but eventually you will need to buy a license once your community grows.

For in-person events, even if you are able to secure a free venue, there are plenty of other costs. This may include catering, building HVAC / security services, cleaning services, or A/V equipment that your venue host or sponsors might not fully cover.

Community organizers often struggle with the question of monetization. This usually comes in the form of event ticketing or community membership fees. The other obvious option is bringing on sponsors to help fund the events and community, something covered in a later chapter.

The question you need to ask yourself is if you are taking time and energy to organize the community, does it make sense to also cover the costs of the community personally? Framed this way, you probably will agree that a nominal ticket or membership fee is a fair exchange of value and is a better path towards long-term sustainability of the community.

Monetization is not a dirty word! Sharing in the costs is simply a reflection of the reality of managing a community and the value that is created as that community grows and scales. Money not only helps take care of all the costs associated with running events, it also allows you to invest further into the community through bigger events, more services, administrative support, and better tools.

The flip side of monetization is that it can also blow up your community. Many would-be communities that had promising starts died when they pushed monetization too hard, too quickly. When members perceive it as a money grab, the backlash leads to a death spiral that destroys the community.

It's a delicate balancing act between revenue and perception. If you put monetization before community, you don't have a community, you just have users. There will be little to sway people to be involved, participate, attend, or share with others.

The monetization decision boils down to one question, what is best for the community? Honesty and transparency are your best means for keeping your motivations oriented towards the good of the community and communicating your intentions. When implementing a fee, bringing on a sponsor, or adding a new revenue stream, be clear with your members as to the value already created by the community, why the need to charge now, and how it benefits the overall community.

To ease into charging fees though, it is recommended that the first event, or first few events, are free for two reasons. In the beginning, when you have no track record, it is easier to convince people to join your events if there is little risk on their end. Even if they do not attend, you have captured their contact information to invite them to future events; this enables you to build up your email list for promotional purposes. The second reason is that you broaden your base of sign-ups that you can later analyze to understand if the types of people registering align to the profiles you want for the community, something discussed more in the chapter on "Curating Membership."

One observation learned early on in the Enterprise Sales Forum was that charging an event fee immediately improved the networking during events. When networking, it is natural that people of similar backgrounds will gather, which is why people attend networking events. You simply feel more relaxed and safer. In that sense, charging acts as a gate that naturally curates the community.

Charging event fees or memberships will lower event attendance initially. Again, if you are transparent about how fees are used for the community, people will understand. Eventually, your numbers will recover and grow because only those people who are truly interested in the community will pay to be involved, creating a flywheel effect that draws other people who value being part of a community with others of similar interests.

At the same time, do not feel pressured to charge fees! There are very legitimate reasons you might not want to charge. If an organization or corporation backs your community, they probably have a mechanism to handle and reimburse your expenses. This is often true for technology user groups that are actively supported by the corporations that wish to see their community thrive.

There are also altruistic reasons to not want to charge. Maybe you simply feel communities should not charge users for anything in the spirit of open source. Perhaps you wish to pay it forward because you have been very successful in your own professional life.

Another common objection to charging is that you may view it as a barrier to accessibility. If inviting students and low-income individuals is important, events fees may be a blocker from attending. However, there is always the option to create lower costs or free tickets that can be clearly advertised to those in financial need.

Lastly, you might prefer the community operate loosely and not get bogged down in operational considerations. Once you start charging money, you get into taxes and bank accounts.. That might require business registration, which leads to legal contracts, and so on. These are all valid concerns and it might be okay to keep things simple.

Whether your reasons are laudable or for convenience, ultimately the most enduring communities are those in which everyone in the community, whether organizers, volunteers, or members, are actively and fairly contributing their fair share. Sharing the burden is what gives a community its backbone.

SOURCING SPEAKERS

There are no strict guidelines when it comes to speaker selection. You can reach out to accomplished individual contributors, notable company executives, industry relevant consultants, well-known book authors, whomever would add value to your community. As the community organizer, you set the rules!

At the Enterprise Sales Forum, the focus is on hosting events that mix networking, sharing, and learning new things in sales. Therefore, choosing relevant speakers with a demonstrated track record of professional excellence in B2B sales is a critical aspect of running worthwhile events. Whomever was brought in to speak, it is always with the goal of providing insights for the community into what really works in modern day B2B sales that is both engaging and practical.

Another aspect to consider for your community is the diversity of your speakers. The Enterprise Sales Forum has an expansive view of diversity to broaden the ideas presented to the community. Speakers from startups and Fortune 500 companies and from a variety of industries such as technology, medical, manufacturing, and media have spoken at events. Diversity is viewed as an opportunity to invite more women and underrepresented groups as speakers so all of the local community's voices have an opportunity to be heard and to inspire others.

As part of your Launch Organizing List, it is suggested to create a separate list for a Speaker Roster. This list will be a valuable resource as you look towards planning the initial set of events. This list should consist of direct connections (i.e., your LinkedIn first-level connections) as well as individuals beyond your existing network whom you believe would be great speakers for your community.

Do not be shy about asking people you do not know to be a speaker. Many successful people you feel would be too busy or important are often more than happy to participate and feel honored to be asked to speak. Everyone has different motivations, whether they view it as an opportunity to recruit, build more brand awareness, or simply to give back to the community. The important point is to ask.

You can be successful in reaching out to people directly on LinkedIn using either an Inmail or a connection request. Feel free to use the following template modified for your specific community:

> Hello [First_Name],
>
> I saw your impressive sales leadership background and wanted to connect. I am the founder of the [Local_Chapter] Enterprise Sales Forum, a community to gather sales pros to share, network & learn. I would love to invite you to speak at a future event. Let me know if you would like to learn more. Thanks!
>
> [Your_Name]

Whatever your approach, short and direct is always best. Also give it some time as your request is not going to be a priority for people. You may need to send a few reminders, send an email, or get an introduction through a common connection to eventually get their attention.

You should also look to your venue hosts, your own company, and your customers for ideas on speakers. The goal is to pull together a list of 20–25 speakers who you can draw from as potential speakers for your first event, as well as for future events.

Before moving to content planning, it is important to reiterate the earlier point about community values as it relates to speakers. There is nothing wrong with speakers having self-interested motivations for speaking at events. This is acceptable and expected since the biggest motivation to speak is to promote something, whether their company, product, or themselves.

While it is not spelled out, speakers are often being asked to contribute their time and expertise freely. Many will do so willingly without any compensation and often will not even ask to expense travel for the event. Despite their willingness to participate, however, your invitation should not be used as a platform for blatant and excessive self-promotion.

The benefit of having clearly defined values for your community is that it provides clear guidelines as to what is and is not acceptable. This also goes for what is the acceptable level of self-promotion by speakers. The values of the Enterprise Sales Forum states it "steers away from overt commercial influence." This does not mean any promotion is forbidden, but it simply has to be in the context of delivering something of value to members first.

When inviting speakers, remember to clearly lay out the ground rules and reiterate the importance of respecting your community values. This will ensure your speakers have the right expectations going in and exiting the event with a positive experience.

PLANNING CONTENT

Once you have a few speakers aligned for the first event, you need to consider format and topics.

The biggest challenge in building a sustainable group is keeping up the momentum. Realistically, you need to plan out at least the first six events. I have found that many other communities lose momentum after the first few events and eventually stop hosting events altogether shortly afterwards. You prevent that by planning out events well in advance and demonstrating momentum.

You might be thinking why identify speakers before deciding content? It is because you can come up with the most compelling list of topics and then realize you might not have people in your network that can contribute as speakers. By building a Speaker Roster first, you see who you have available to build a list of topics around and then invite speakers based on their strengths.

The first consideration is format. The most effective format, which the Enterprise Sales Forum has used most often, is the **hosted panel** event. In this structure, 2-4 speakers are invited for an interview style conversation on a planned topic moderated by one of the community organizers. The moderator asks a series of questions as well as invites the audience to ask questions of the panelists.

Other options for formats include fireside chats, presentations, and roundtables.

- The **fireside chat** is most effective when you have a prominent guest speaker, such as a CEO, book author, or well-known business leader. This is an interview style format requiring questions from a moderator and a good rapport between the speaker and moderator.

- ⬚ The **presentation** is an educational format in which the speaker teaches on a topic. This often works if the material is "dense," meaning it involves lots of analysis, processes, and tactics. Presentations can be effective when given by a notable speaker who comes with a proven and effective presentation.

- ⬚ The **roundtable** is an immersive format in which you have fewer attendees that are all invited to participate in an interactive question and discussion experience. These formats do not necessitate a speaker, but are best when you already have a well-established community and want to target a niche audience such as people at a certain experience level or expertise.

Coupled with format is content. The most logical source for discussion topics and content would be events hosted by other similar groups. You should also follow trending topics that are discussed in online groups and webinars. These are good sources for topical content that most speakers would have strong opinions on and would likely be of interest to your community.

It is also recommended to ask the speakers you reach out to for their ideas. They most likely have a few topics they are passionate about and have some relevant stories and lessons to share. To make this productive though, suggest a few topics that might be relevant based on their experience as possibilities, then ask:

- ⬚ What most excites you or gets you most fired up about X topic?
- ⬚ What have been some really difficult challenges you solved recently?
- ⬚ Where do you see your industry being most in need of fixing?

This should elicit one or two good content topics. Once a topic is selected, you will need to create a captivating title for the event / talk, write a short three sentence synopsis of the talk, and 10-12 questions to ask the speaker(s) during the talk (if it is a panel or interview style discussion).

PROMOTING COMMUNITY

Once you have a venue, speaker(s), and a topic arranged, you can begin to promote the community and event. First, you need to create an event page and then seed the community and event with relevant members who are engaged and invested with passion for a community of peers.

The Event Page is the central online location for directing people towards in order to join the community and register for events. You want to find a solution that is easy to use for organizing and easy for your members. In the past, most groups started with Meetup.com. For the purposes of the Enterprise Sales Forum, however, a combination of Eventbrite and Mailchimp are used along with a built-in integration to synchronize the member lists. There are many options available if you search for community and event platforms. The key is to find something free or close to free in order to minimize your costs.

Regardless of platform choice, you need to create the event splash page. This page would include event title, event description, speaker bio(s), venue, date/time, directions, agenda, social sharing links, special notes, and any photos, such as pictures of the speaker(s) or banner images to promote the event. Once the page is set up, save the page URL for your promotion messages.

Once the event page is published, the community then needs to be seeded with members. Again, having an established network of local leaders and professionals helps. Try extracting your LinkedIn connections and address book to build an initial seeding list. Do not worry if not everyone in your list is necessarily relevant to your community, as you are going to make a general announcement. This is an example of a template used by the

Enterprise Sales Forum that you are free to modify and use in your initial outreach:

> Need Help – the [Local_Chapter] Enterprise Sales Forum

> Hello [First_Name],

> I wanted to share a group I started called the [Local_Chapter] Enterprise Sales Forum, a community to bring sales professionals together to share, network, & learn. Our first event is [Date] featuring a talk by [Speaker(s)]. Here is the link to the event page:

> [Event_page_URL]

> Would you mind sharing this with your friends and colleagues in sales? Thanks!

> [Your_Name]

With just your personal outreach alone, you should have a decent number of sign-ups for your first event. In the weeks leading up to the event, send a few more reminders about the event to the same list. As in sales, persistence is key and often people will miss the first, second, or third emails. If you are curious as to what tools to use in order to manage this process, please see the Appendix – Email Merge Technologies.

In tandem with your direct outreach, there may be a select group of key influencers, connectors, and motivated individuals you will want to help spread the word. To leverage this influential audience, create a Launch Packet for your supporters that contains easy to share snippets (sample tweets, links to event pages, videos, or photos, etc.) about your community that can be shared across multiple channels. Think of email, relevant social networks, IM/messaging channels, etc. The Launch Packet does not have to be a long document, in fact shorter is sweeter. Also, the easier you make it to share by adding one-click shareable links and embeddable media, the higher your response rates will be in having your initial group of supporters share your posts.

Once you have created the Launch Packet, you can modify it to create a Promotion Packet for promoting future events. You can include your initial supporters from the launch in the distribution, but also include your speakers, the venue hosts, sponsors, influencers, and volunteers.

On subsequent outreach efforts after the first event, you can narrow your outreach focus to the core audience. While going narrow is good, reaching out to groups and people who might be complementary to your group, even if it is not your exact audience, is also important. A good example specific to the Enterprise Sales Forum is including marketing people in the outreach because they interact so closely with sales teams and know enough sales professionals with whom to share the community.

In terms of outreach, I believe LinkedIn is the best network to leverage for finding potential new members. You can also join other groups with an online presence that would likely have members similarly interested in a community you are building and use the messaging features to selectively invite people to join your group. Lastly, industry associations can be a good source to draw from if you can gain access to a membership list or have a way to message members directly.

Conversely, there are certain groups who should be discouraged from joining the community. It is suggested you not invite people who would seek to actively sell and pitch members, which diminishes from the quality of the community you are building. If there are people who have joined the community who you feel do not reflect the spirit of the community, do not hesitate to remove those individuals. The success of the community is very much built on social capital, strong word of mouth, and the belief that the group is built with and for peers.

As you promote, consider partnering with other communities that can also actively promote your community through their distribution channels. By sharing your community and events through their website, newsletter, social media accounts, and other announcement mechanisms, that has a strong influence in drawing new members. Always look for opportunities for increasing the visibility of your community by working with prominent business leaders, executives, influencers, and media outlets.

As the community begins to take shape and the member list grows, measure the success of your outreach efforts. Which communication channels are most effective? Which partners draw the most new members? What is the right cadence in terms of connecting with members about upcoming events and other news? Your success in creating a vibrant, energized, and growing community will in part depend on balancing persistent awareness with the danger of overcommunication. Therefore, throttle your efforts as appropriate so you do not risk needlessly losing members due to incessant messaging.

Before leaving this chapter though, it is critical to share the single most important aspect of promotion:

ALWAYS BE PROMOTING

I can guarantee you will have a strong and thriving community if you approach this mantra religiously. Never slack in reaching out to new members and connecting with existing members. Always find opportunities to share the community with people you know. Include your community information in your email signature, drop it into conversations, add your community as a job on your LinkedIn profile, and actively tweet and post about the community. Mention the group in online forums and chat rooms and invite people to join. *Always promote.*

CURATING MEMBERSHIP

When first launching a community, you are often not picky when it comes to who joins. Getting anyone to pay attention often seems like a triumph. Perhaps you have the opposite experience though and already have a large following, so you are not as concerned, as you have plenty of people in your community. The main reason many community organizers are not particular is because the idea of curating who can join often has a negative perception, the proverbial velvet rope at a nightclub.

I view curating membership as the work organizers do in order to build a stronger community in two respects:

- **Diversity & Inclusion** – Championing a culture that is open and accepting of all backgrounds, cultures, and experiences.

- **Safety & Serendipity** – Fostering trust and openness among people of similar interests to create greater value, innovation, and opportunity.

On the surface, you may feel these are opposing ideas. On one hand, you want to promote a more diverse membership, while also declaring membership is not for everyone; on the contrary, you will mold your community to be stronger by using these concepts.

Diversity & Inclusion

The reason diversity is important is that a diverse community is a community that innovates. There have been numerous studies demonstrating the upside of diversity[3]. Bringing people together with different experiences broadens the approaches to solving problems, spurs on new ideas, and challenges assumptions and biases we have in ways a homogenous group cannot.

What exactly is meant by diversity? The word will have a different emphasis depending on where in the world you are, but the Enterprise Sales Forum views diversity as including differences in gender, race, language, culture, religion, sexual orientation, age, disability, and national origin. It can also include differences in experience based on background, education, and income. Collectively, this creates a community that is reflective of our global reality.

Diversity alone is not enough though. You also need to create a welcoming experience so those joining the community, no matter their background, feel included and respected to the same degree as any other member of the community. This is not an easy thing to accomplish, as we tend to gravitate towards those with whom we have similar backgrounds, physical traits, or cultural characteristics.

By making a concerted effort towards curating a community to be diverse and inclusive, you are starting the slow process that will result in change. When the Enterprise Sales Forum began, its events were sometimes upwards of 90% male and over 95% white. Guest speakers were all white and only one female speaker had presented by that point.

The Enterprise Sales Forum took three steps to address the lack of diversity head on:

- **Bring on Influencers** – Specifically created diverse panels that featured underrepresented people and women and asked those speakers to promote to their own networks.

---

[3] "Why Diverse Teams Are Smarter" https://hbr.org/2016/11/why-diverse-teams-are-smarter

- **Build Specific Content** – Created specific events like Diversity Talks and Women in Sales Month to elevate the topic to the community.

- **Direct Outreach** – Searched LinkedIn and specifically invited women as well as Black, Latinx, and Asian sales leaders to attend the event.

The combination of influence, content, and outreach was used to curate a more diverse community that otherwise might never change by itself. Now the community is significantly more balanced both from a speaker and an attendee perspective, which helps to create more inviting events.

The efforts to focus on diversity also had the side effect of increasing the diversity of the organizing teams. This broadened our perspectives as a team and helped us to be better at calling out biases in content creation and programs being created for the members. Do not forget to consider how diverse your organizing team is when building your community.

Safety & Serendipity

At some point, you need to be honest with how open you want your community to be. The growth of any community depends on the willingness of people with similar interests to come together to learn, share, and connect.

This is how the magic of serendipity works. When you know you are in a place among peers, people let their guards down and are more willing to network freely and meet new people. This creates the perfect environment for ideas to come together, for collaboration to occur, and for relationships to be forged. This is all due to the calibrated randomness of a curated community.

Serendipity is quick to evaporate though. Suppose you go to an event for software developers and half of the people you meet are dentists. That is not the most positive experience (unless you have tooth pain and need a dentist). The expectation of people in the community is that they will meet others like themselves, creating psychological safety that encourages more sharing and engagement.

One of the principles of the Enterprise Sales Forum is to be open and welcoming. However, that does not mean the community is open to everyone. The community makes it clear that it is a community dedicated to B2B sales professionals. In the early days, I just accepted anyone who signed up to attend events because I felt growing the Meetup.com membership number was an important measure of success.

Turns out, the number of members is a poor metric when determining community health. When I analyzed the membership, at least one-quarter of the members were not in B2B sales. There were recruiters and financial planners and random signups from people addicted to signing up to meetup groups. Nevertheless, that analysis showed many technical startup founders were looking to learn about selling, so this also had a positive outcome of expanding promotion to a group the community could serve.

In the early days of your community, do not spend as much energy tightly curating membership. People naturally self-select if you clearly name your community and describe events for your intended audience to understand who you serve and the type of content they should expect. For the Enterprise Sales Forum, it is clear from the name who the community serves. If it was named the "Big Dollars Society" or had events with titles like "Open Networking Night," no one would have any idea what the community was about or who should join.

Instead, monitor and observe the early events. If there are people who attend events who are disruptive or make others uncomfortable, you have every right as the organizer to ban those individuals. The Code of Conduct is discussed in the Appendix, but for now understand the safety and well-being of your community come first.

Once you have completed some events, you should review the data on past signups and the people on the membership list to see if you need to curate the community more actively. There are a few options at your disposal:

- **Reinforcement**: Communicate the mission often to encourage self-deselection
- **Monetize**: Charge fees to encourage self-deselection
- **Shadow ban**: Remove the person from event promotion and communication channels
- **Unregister**: Remove the person from event registration

- ▢ **Location Masking**: Only make event address / URL available to curated group
- ▢ **Outright ban**: Remove person completely from community

The best and least confrontational method for curation is allowing members to remove themselves through self-deselection. By making it very explicit who the community serves, those who are not among that group will generally get the message that the community is not for them.

Removing people and hiding information is less ideal, but necessary in some circumstances. There was one person in particular that kept attending the Boston chapter events for the Enterprise Sales Forum. He was an oddball who would leave weird messages in online discussion groups, ask inappropriate questions at events, and made nearly everyone he interacted with uncomfortable. After he attended three events in which I set ticket fees, hid the location, and deleted him from mailings, I removed him outright and alerted building security.

These are the unpleasant moments of running a community, but the vast amount of the time will be positive and uplifting. Curating your community is an opportunity to build a stronger community and stronger connections that otherwise would never happen. While all of the recommendations and advice provided here is critical for long-term community success, the most important job of the community organizer is to bring together people that most value connecting with others of similar interests.

SECURING SPONSORS

While every community will have their own set of core goals, for the most part it boils down to creating value for its members and generating great content. But for that to happen on a consistent basis, the community must be self-sustaining. This means the community needs to generate some revenue at a minimum to cover cost, either through event ticket sales or through sponsorships.

Before going farther, it is important to emphasize that money is not evil! Asking for money in exchange for attending an event or accessing your community is an acceptable practice. First, it covers costs for the community, since even free venues and software often do not adequately account for all costs. Second, revenue is the fuel that allows you to offer even more value to your community, to invest more of your time, and to grow your organization to support more services for your members. Karma points and accolades are certainly welcome, but running a community ultimately requires cash.

Monetization via ticket sales and membership fees was discussed in a prior chapter, so let's change the focus to adding revenue through sponsorships. The benefit of sponsors is they can offer more financial support on a consistent basis. This allows you to plan ahead since you know you have a set amount of working capital. Sponsorships also let you subsidize ticket and membership fees at a reasonable rate to encourage more signups.

However, you should view sponsors as an opportunity to add value to your community, rather than just financial backing. Sponsors can provide resources that further learning or enhance some aspect of the community experience. In that way, sponsors are truly a partner in contributing to the growth of the community. Therefore, you should evaluate each opportunity to bring on a sponsor using the following criteria:

- **Clearly stated motivations and objectives in joining the community**
- **Logical fit to the purpose and goals of your community**
- **Alignment to the vision and values of your community**
- **Commitment to active participation and sharing with your community**
- **Strong bias for excellence and thought leadership in their industry**

These criteria will help guide your decision process and ensure you are partnering with worthwhile organizations that value your community and members. If there is a question on even one of these criteria, pause and take time to ask the questions to make sure you and your potential sponsor see eye to eye on the value of working together and the importance to members of the community.

Likewise, you want to ensure sponsors find value in their investment into your community. Your commitment to sponsors as a valued partner can be viewed in the following four ways:

- **Raising market awareness**
- **Elevating their thought leadership**
- **Connecting with talented job seekers**
- **Opening business development opportunities**

The types of organizations that make most sense as sponsors will vary widely based on the community and its needs. Common types of sponsors include business services firms (law firms, accountants, banks, etc.), technology companies that provide relevant solutions, training/coaching companies, recruitment agencies, sales/marketing agencies, etc. Other potential sponsors include your venue host(s), companies actively hiring, and companies looking to expand into the local market. All are viable options if they abide by the five criteria above and you can make it worthwhile for the sponsor.

How many sponsors is best? It depends on your needs. You do not want to look like a NASCAR equivalent of a community with hundreds of logos.

Plus, it would be nearly impossible to manage. The ideal arrangement is to have 2-3 local sponsors signed up for long-term sponsorship packages. The focus is on long-term (quarterly, half-year, or yearly) because it is easier to manage, provides a dependable revenue stream, and sponsorships take time to develop. The value for a sponsor usually does not take shape until a few months into the partnership.

Sponsor promotion takes the form of mentions through various assets that you create in support of the community. Those assets include the events you host, your website, the event sign-up page, event announcements, newsletter, and social media. Where appropriate, you can also offer a speaking slot to sponsors and share high quality sponsor content through your community communications channels.

How much should you charge for sponsorships? Again, it all depends on what is needed to sustain your community. The other factors are market forces and the value you can provide sponsors. Do not be reluctant in asking for what you believe your community is worth. You can also tier your sponsorship levels so you offer higher value and exposure for a sponsor who is willing to pay more. Most sponsor packages are structured with three or four commitment levels of increasing value and worth. This way, you can bring on smaller sponsors that may pay a few hundred a month to larger sponsors that can pay many thousands a month for access and exposure to your community.

MANAGING EVENTS

It's the big day, your first event! Now it is showtime, where all the hard work and effort comes together. In order to ensure it runs smoothly requires thorough planning and preparation to deliver a positive experience for all participants.

This is where having someone in the role Head of Events really matters most. While community and events are a team effort, one person should have the ownership, authority, and accountability to ensure the logistics of the event are in place for a successful outcome.

The Head of Events also happens to be the most collaborative role of the team. The events team needs input from sponsors regarding venue and from content to understand speaker and presentation requirements. They also coordinate closely with promotions on aspects of event logistics to be communicated and to determine the expected number of attendees.

What makes the Head of Events the most important and most complex of any role though is all about precision and execution. Once speakers, content, and venue is booked, the Head of Events brings it all together to ensure a high quality event experience.

The best way to keep all the details together is to create a checklist. This checklist is not a one and done effort, but something that will evolve over time or spawn multiple versions based on the type of event. Two examples of checklists from the Enterprise Sales Forum are included in the Appendix as a good starting point for developing your own. Also, create a shared, online version so the whole team can be up to speed, receive task assignments, and get notifications on event status.

The rest of this chapter examines specific tasks and considerations that have led to successful in-person and virtual event experiences. Use these concepts as guides to explore rather than a paint-by-numbers book. The context and situation of events and communities vary widely. Some things will be universally applicable, like sorting out the restroom situation and creating an event page. Other things are not necessary but are strongly encouraged, such as Wi-Fi access and food and beverage. Then there are things like a Jobs Board and Social Media that are not important in the grand scheme of the event but can add to the attendee experience.

Because of the rise in virtual events since 2020, the content has been separated into in-person events and virtual events. The topics of multiple languages and accessibility are addressed separately, given the complexity of supporting those requirements.

MANAGING IN-PERSON EVENTS

Once the first event has been scheduled and promoted, it is time to consider the logistics of running the events. Over the course of hosting many events across multiple communities, below are considerations that have been found to lead to hosting successful events.

Pre-Event Setup

- ☐ **Scheduling:** Events hosted in the evenings on a monthly cadence tend to be easier to schedule and attend. That does not exclude morning or lunchtime events, but you need to be aware of what your members prefer and can accommodate. Remember, they are taking time out of their busy schedules to participate in your community. It is also recommended to keep event dates on the same time during the month so it becomes a regular thing for members to schedule ahead of time. As for dates, Tuesday, Wednesday, or Thursday are the best days for hosting events. Worst case, Monday evenings or Friday breakfast meetings can be considered, but these are not ideal.

- ☐ **Agenda:** Two hours is generally a good amount of time, with the first hour being networking and the second hour being the talk/panel/presentation. This provides plenty of time for talking and learning without feeling rushed or over-extended. However, this will depend on the time of day of the event (two hours is generally hard to schedule for breakfast and lunch events), and the types of programs and events that work best for your community.

- **Speaker Preparation:** Create a Speaker Packet for each speaker that contains event logistics (where, when, agenda), social sharing snippets, and format / questions for the event if it is a panel or fireside chat. Also, keep actively in touch with speakers to ensure they show up on time and at the right location. A week before the event, set up a pre-event call to review the Speaker Packet and questions.

- **Key Roles:** As the founder of the community, you might fall into the trap of thinking you are responsible for running the event, moderating the speakers, and being the master of ceremonies (MC). It is recommended you recruit others to help you (see "Building the Team" chapter) so you can split the roles and switch off between being the event manager, MC, and moderator.

  o **Event Manager** – Makes sure the event runs smoothly, liaises with the venue host, ensures check-in runs smoothly, and directs the volunteers.

  o **Master of Ceremonies (MC)** – Gets people seated, kicks off and closes out the event, makes sponsor and community announcements. Also helps with photos, social media sharing, and passing the mic around to audience members during the Q&A time. Then concludes the event with some closing remarks such as the next event and after-party location.

  o **Moderator** – Responsible for preparing the speaker(s) and conducting the content section of the event. They not only ask questions, but also manage questions from the audience.

- **Volunteers:** It is highly advised for you to ask a couple of people to help check-in guests and provide general assistance during the event, from greeting guests to taking photos to assisting with social media or lending a hand with other setup needs. Make sure to coordinate with volunteers well-ahead of time with what you need, and thank them afterwards for their assistance. Over time, you can create a Volunteer Roster of people who wish to be actively involved in your community and you can call upon as needed.

- **Event Pages:** As the focus is on building community, leveraging a community-oriented platform is suggested. The most popular is Eventbrite, which is free for organizers and integrates to many platforms. There are also many other simple alternatives, such as Meetup.com, that have more community-oriented features. Once you build scale in your community, there are many other community-specific platforms that can provide more functionality and flexibility. Take note of multilingual and accessibility issues as well when creating the event pages, as discussed later in this chapter.

- **Ticketing:** This is part and parcel to Event Pages to enable you to have people formally register for the event. The other side of ticketing is charging an attendance fee. The Enterprise Sales Forum has found that initially charging for attending events can be a challenge, as the community has no scale or credibility yet. Therefore, focus on drawing as wide and large of an audience as possible, and NOT charging for events initially. Once the group reaches a certain scale, there are various options for turning on paid ticketing on your chosen event page/ ticketing system.

- **Ticketing Information:** In a community of any size, there will be people with food restrictions, food allergies, and even attendees with disabilities. Create an open text field in the ticket registration flow for attendees to indicate special needs for themselves or person(s) they are inviting along, and make sure to account for that in the event planning process (such as wheelchair accessibility).

- **Privacy and Data Protection:** At any community event, photos and video are almost always taken. This should be expected by any attendee; therefore, make this known to those signing up. In the registration process, include a statement clarifying the use of photography and/or video mediums as well as how the community will use the information collected. Additionally, make it explicit that such information will not be shared with other parties without direct permission.

Event Venue Setup

- **Seating:** There needs to be enough seating for the number of attendees you expect. You want to create the sense of a full room, so avoid putting out more chairs than attendees. You also need a few chairs for the panelists / speakers in the front. Adjust accordingly based on the size of the community and the events you host. Some hosts/venues may not have enough seats available, but there are usually places to rent chairs for events that you can share with your event host(s).

- **Green Room:** Setup an area where the speakers and event team can assemble and chat prior to the event that is away from the attendees. This brief period to bring together speakers before the event improves the rapport of the group and the quality of discussion, even for the more experienced speakers. If you are tight for space, find a quiet corner and corral the speakers together, preferably before attendees start arriving in large numbers, so the speakers can mingle and engage with the attendees.

- **Food & Beverages:** You should arrange with your venue host to provide beverages (alcoholic and non-alcoholic) and food. Stick with appetizer-style foods and be considerate of various food concerns, such as religious requirements, dietary needs, and vegetarian options. If another sponsor is covering food and drink (like a caterer), coordinate who is purchasing and arranging for delivery. Worst case scenario, there are various online services now available for convenient food and beverage delivery if you are responsible for ordering. An important point is to have all food items and beverages labeled with food allergen and restriction information.

- **Audio/Visual:** Your venue host should provide the appropriate audio and presentation equipment. Using a projection system or large screen to share slides is a good idea. It is also helpful to use an auto-advancing presentation with information about the event, social sharing information, sponsors, and speakers. Additionally, for presentation-style events in which videos may be played, having the ability to connect a laptop to a sound system is helpful. As for audio, wireless mics (handheld or lavaliere, either works) and a high-quality PA system for sound projection are advisable, both so the audience can clearly hear the speakers and so any recorded video has adequate sound amplification. Note that most company audio setups will have a limited number of mics, so you may need to instruct your panelists to share mics during the panel discussion.

- **Video & Photography:** Both of these mediums are necessary for events. Visual assets provide social proof of your community and get people excited for your next event(s). But if you are going to invest time and money in photos and video, you should also make sure your venue has adequate sound and lighting quality. At first, you and your limited team will probably be taking the pictures and filming the talks, but in time you can have volunteers help or even hire professionals to handle photos and videos (if you have the financial wherewithal).

- **Social Media:** The other way to build social proof is to have people talk about your community and events as they are happening. Create a unique hashtag that is easy to type and unique from other hashtags (do a quick search beforehand to make sure your hashtag is not in use). Then this tag can be used for posts to various social media platforms to be shared, liked, retweeted, etc. This is also an easy way to amplify your video and photo efforts and engage your community to create content such as photos, short videos, and audio clips during the event.

- **Interactive Feeds:** Set up a visual display or presentation screen off to the side to rotate interesting information during the event, such as following the event Twitter hashtag, posting interactive polls and Q&A via apps, and upcoming events or member testimonials. Rather than being distracting, it offers a useful visual contrast to the aural content of the speakers and it heightens the engagement of the event. This can be setup with another laptop and either a large display or projector, where a volunteer rotates through content (or can also be automated with some ingenuity if you are technically inclined).

- **Jobs Board:** A big motivator for many to attend events is to find new opportunities or to connect with potential new hires. Make it easy for attendees to connect and add a whiteboard, easel, or other flat surface where attendees can post job openings for job seekers to read. Let attendees know ahead of time as well, and then at the event have a "Jobs Board" sign with a pile of large-sized sticky notes and markers for attendees to start posting. Encourage greeters and the team handling sign-ins to also remind attendees of the resource.

75

- **Live Broadcasting:** One way to combine the power of video with social media while providing an invaluable service to your members is to live broadcast your events. There are enterprise platforms like Livestream (which is what the Enterprise Sales Forum uses), but you can use free services such as Periscope and Facebook Live to stream your events in real-time and share those links with your audience. This promotes even more online engagement and is an added benefit for community members who cannot attend an event in person.

- **Wi-Fi Access:** Reliable and fast wireless connectivity *is a must*. The Enterprise Sales Forum uses Wi-Fi for check-in software and live broadcasting of events. You will also have the same needs if you decide to live broadcast or use any cloud-based systems. The other purpose of Wi-Fi is to improve the guest experience for attendees, which also encourages social sharing.

- **Restrooms:** Make it easy for attendees to access the restrooms. Sometimes these facilities require a code or keycard access, so arrange for unrestricted access to restrooms for the duration of the event.

- **Security:** Most buildings require check-in at a front desk before proceeding to the office hosting your event. Make sure to coordinate with your hosts about when you need to provide guest lists. A good rule of thumb is to submit the list by 12 PM the day of the event (depending on the time of your event as well), but requirements can vary from building to building. If there is no building security, it is likely the doors automatically lock. Therefore, make accommodations to allow attendees to freely enter the building during the hours of the event.

- **Employee Contact:** Due to liability issues, it is important that at least one employee of the venue host be present throughout the course of the event who can aid with equipment or handle issues at the venue.

- **Directions, Mass Transit, & Parking:** To ensure your members can find events without issues, you should share venue directions as well as parking garage locations (preferably low-cost or validated options) with the community. Also encouraged is on-site directions and signs to help attendees find their way once they arrive at the location.

☐ **Setup and Clean-up:** As with seating, you should rely upon your host venue to provide services for setting up the venue, from arranging chairs to operating AV equipment, and to clean-up and put the venue in order after the completion of the event. Do not just rely upon the venue for clean-up though. It is your job as a community leader to do your part in keeping the venue clean and orderly, which will increase your chances of using that venue in the future.

MANAGING VIRTUAL EVENTS

In terms of pre-event planning, many of the considerations stated for in-person events remain the same. However, the logistics for running virtual events are quite different. Since 2020, many community managers realize in the switch from in-person events to virtual, there are a new set of challenges and contingencies to plan for. Below are some of the key things to think about when hosting virtual events.

- **Event Hosting Platform:** The most critical aspect of a virtual event experience is ensuring the platform you choose works well. This means all participants, including attendees, speakers, volunteers, and organizers, can access the content and all aspects of the event easily and without appreciable loss in quality (given reasonable bandwidth at the participant's end). The software is the entirety of your event experience. It is not just the location, it is also the rooms, the A/V, the seating, the transit, etc. Therefore, it is critical to do tests, dry runs, and allocate extra time in the event schedule for setup and configuration purposes.

- **Audio/Visual:** Issues with audio and video quality will have a much greater impact on the event experience than in-person events. Ensure all speakers, presenters, and MCs have an acceptable microphone, headphones, and webcam setup and a strong Wi-Fi signal. It is best to start the event 15 minutes earlier for speakers and presenters to test equipment prior to the official start of the event.

- **Content Format:** Most online events in the past were generally static webinars. You had a panel or presenter with pre-recorded content and little to no interactive features to the event. Based on the platform you choose these days, there is much more flexibility. Consider if you are going to do an event that is more like a webinar or one with various sessions, such as a mix of a presentation and panel, a free-form discussion, or a moderated conversation. Whatever the format, ensure your content fits the format and have any screenshares, apps, videos, audio, or presentations loaded and tested beforehand.

▸ **Sessions:** Many community-oriented events keep things simple with networking and a talk or panel discussion. In the virtual world, you have the flexibility of adding multi-track sessions, breakrooms, and networking time (based on the functionality of the chosen platform). Decide if you want to provide a different and more interactive experience with multiple sessions or keep things simple with a single-track event.

▸ **Audience Size:** The number of attendees you plan to have will play a significant factor in how you organize the agenda and content. First, there are cost considerations, such as a maximum number of attendees based on the software license. Second is the logistics and maintaining engagement. With a larger audience, you will need more volunteers to help to handle questions and audience participation. Also, it is harder to corral attendees into breakout rooms if you are running a multi-session event. Understand how that flow works in your event software and run scenarios to make sure you are able to transition smoothly between sessions.

▸ **Engagement Tools:** The chosen software platform will most likely have various tools allowing you to engage with the attendees. The most basic level is messaging built into every platform to have a dialogue, share information, or ask and answer questions. More advanced features built into some tools include dedicated Q&A features, polls, quizzes, and ability to create small groups. There are also options to use third party tools and many communities maintain a Slack channel or Discord server for the community to share and collaborate on. Then there are also tools like Slido that offer up dedicated polling and Q&A features. Whatever you choose, make sure there are organizers and/or volunteers available during the event to monitor activity and to engage as needed.

- **Social Media:** Because the event is completely online, social media plays an even more critical role. Though you may want to focus engagement in the tools provided by the event hosting platform, do not neglect the audience NOT attending your event. This gives those not able to attend a rundown and recap of the highlights of the event. Since the events are online and recorded, you can use the event video and photos as assets to your social media following.

- **Video & Photography:** This takes on a very different meaning in a virtual environment since the entire body of content is recorded by default. Therefore, it is easy to transfer video to whatever content store you use, whether YouTube, Vimeo, or another site. Photography might appear less important in a virtual setting. However, one interesting engagement method observed is events asking attendees to send screenshots of themselves to the organizers. Likewise, taking screenshots of the panel/ speakers is also a good way to remember the panel and have assets you can then share via social media.

- **Volunteers:** Calling on volunteers to help during online events means taking on different roles in the virtual world. The best use of volunteers in this environment is to help with the flow of online activities, such as facilitating Q&A, sending out polls, and being active over the online chat and social media. Designate a volunteer Engagement Squad and assign specific tasks to lead during the event so the organizing team can focus on overall event quality.

- **Platform Support:** What happens if the event hosting platform experiences issues that affect event quality? Do you have a chat room, email, or call center that you can contact for immediate assistance? Make sure you have ready access to help in an emergency and have a backup plan should the chosen platform fail.

Giving thought to platform support cannot be overstated. The most important insight communities are learning from running virtual events is to always have a backup plan. For the Enterprise Sales Forum, that backup has been Zoom, given that the more robust event platform options are still maturing.

Your choice of in-person events venue is generally dependable. There are weather conditions and emergencies that can cause cancellations, but those are very rare occurrences. A virtual event is completely dependent on the software provider, so if that provider should experience scalability or reliability issues during an event, you are mostly out of luck. Always prepare and have a Plan B ready when those situations arise.

ADDITIONAL EVENT CONSIDERATIONS

Multi-Language Considerations

When planning an event, what is the main language people in the community speak and that the content will be delivered in? Do you plan to support multiple languages? One of the toughest tasks for any event organizer is to manage an event that needs to support more than one language.

To make things simpler, choose the local language of the prospective bulk of attendees to be the main language for the community. It is important to make the members of your community feel as welcome as possible, and language is one of the biggest factors in making a community feel safe.

As your community builds, reevaluate this decision and see if there are valid reasons for making the community more inclusive to other language speakers. For example, cities that have a large number of highly skilled foreign workers/ expats could make for excellent speakers, valued volunteers, and enthusiastic members of the community.

If you do decide to support multiple languages, ask yourself the following:

- ▢ What languages will need to be supported?
- ▢ Do you need to translate speaker content and presentation?
- ▢ How will presentation materials and other assets be translated?
- ▢ Who among your attendees needs translation services?
- ▢ What equipment will you require?
- ▢ Who will provide real-time translation services?
- ▢ How will your event costs change based on translation needs?

- ▢ Would translation be required just for events or for all community needs?
- ▢ Does adding multi-language align to the vision for your community?

Being multi-language can be a valuable service. It is also a time consuming and costly service. Therefore, be certain the members in the community also believe adding languages to be beneficial to them. Given the extra effort entailed, this is not a decision to jump into lightly.

Accessibility Considerations

When organizing events, we tend to think of planning and managing from our own perspectives. This is why diversity is so critical in helping to broaden those perspectives. If your events are going to be truly inclusive and represent the diversity of the community, it is important to also consider your event's accessibility.

Accessibility in the broad sense means the design of products, devices, services, or environments are usable by people with disabilities. Laws supporting accessibility will differ based on country and jurisdiction. In the United States, as an example, accessibility is governed by the Americans with Disabilities Act, ensuring access to public accommodations and those with disabilities can have full and equal enjoyment of facilities. This means considering accessibility from the moment someone finds your community website or registration page to the actual venue itself, whether in-person or online.

Accessibility also covers a wide range of disabilities. There are visual impairments, hearing impairments, mobility impairments as well as cognitive impairments. Each of these groups has specific needs that will need to be accommodated in order to fully value the event experience.

This all can seem daunting when just starting a community, as it is difficult enough just ensuring the first few events are run without incident. With limited resources, money, and time, how can you support a truly accessible and inclusive community with the proper accommodations at events?

Let's cover the key areas in the event planning process where accessibility concerns will arise.

Website

The very first exposure people will have of your community will most likely be the website you host your events on for promotion and registration. You may even have your own website. If you are using other services for hosting events, there is a high likelihood these services will have undergone testing for accessibility already and have a statement regarding their accessibility on their website. If you are ever in doubt, there are free utilities available that test websites for the most common issues that arise, such as screen reader compatibility and compliance with Web Content Accessibility Guidelines 2.1 (WCAG 2.1) and WAI-ARIA.

It can be overwhelming to go through all of the recommendations. The point, however, is not to immerse yourself in the details, but to be aware of potential accessibility issues that might arise with the site you have chosen for event hosting. If you have your own website, or plan to down the road, be aware of WCAG, WAI-ARIA, and screen reader compliance as you evaluate vendors for designing and building your site. If they are not aware of these standards, it is highly unlikely they will be able to deliver a site that meets minimal accessibility requirements.

Event Page

Even if the website you use, or your own website, is accessible, that does not mean the page promoting your event is accessible. Here are a few things to keep in mind:

- Reduce the amount of text where sensible to do so (i.e., reduce speaker bios, shorten descriptions, use bulleted lists vs. paragraphs);

- Add details on accessibility, such as transportation, parking, venue, etc. (see below);

- Add text for image descriptions either in the image itself or as a caption;

- Add captions and post full transcriptions for video and audio media;

- Ensure contrast of text is high enough so text is easily readable;

- Create headings of different sizes for denoting structure and meaning;
- Consider eliminating extra steps in the sign up process and lengthening timeouts on registration; and
- Include an accessibility statement about your event(s) and services provided (i.e., sign language).

Finally, if people do have issues with website accessibility, address the concern or provide an alternative path to access the site. Inclusiveness starts with serving the needs of everyone in your community when they need the extra support.

Transportation

Be aware of how people with disabilities will travel to the event. Are the public transportation options accessible with ramps, guide rails, elevators, etc.? You can find out from the website of the transportation provider. If driving, what is the parking situation? Ask the venue host for information or search for local garages that clearly state they are accessible. Once you have these details, communicate that on your event page, in email communications, and all other notification channels to members.

Venue

For in-person events, the venue can pose many questions, and challenges. In some countries, the law stipulates that public spaces, including workplaces, businesses, event venues, and the like, need to accommodate people with disabilities. In practice, that does not always translate into options that are convenient or well-communicated.

The person in charge of the upcoming event, the Events Manager, should be on the lookout for the following things when doing a walk-through of any venue host:

- Ramps, automatic doors, and elevators to enter the building (from outside or parking structure);
- Ability to navigate to the event room/area and common areas used during the event;

- Spaces that are wide enough to navigate through and within the venue;

- Room for seating that accommodates wheelchairs, service pets, and companions;

- Transition points, doorways, terrain, or pathways with obstacles that prevent movement; and

- Access to restrooms is unobstructed and proper accessible fittings such as grab bars and automatic sinks are in place.

As with transportation, include any information on accessibility that should be communicated ahead of time so that those needing accessibility options can plan and prepare.

Event

During the event, there are situations that can limit inclusiveness, which the Event Manager should be looking out for, including:

- **Signage** - Signs to direct attendees should be clear and fonts large enough

- **Sign Language** - Decide if you will have sign language interpreters at event

- **Food Labels** - Clearly label food and identify potential allergens or restrictions

- **Seating** - Ensure space is reserved to accommodate wheelchairs & helpers

- **Service Animals** - Determine if facilities are needed for service animals

- **Volunteers** - Instruct volunteers on do's and don'ts of helping those with disabilities

An important point regarding volunteers, community leaders, and all people involved in supporting the event is to be helpful and respectful to those with disabilities. It is easy to be overly helpful, so keep an eye out, ask before helping, and be willing to assist where needed.

Virtual Events

When the event is virtual, it eases some of the preparation needed since transportation, venue, and in-person event considerations no longer apply. That does not mean accessibility is not a concern, however. Just as with the website, there are online tools used to host your events that need to be assessed for accessibility.

Whatever platform you decide to use, make sure those with disabilities will be able to navigate and enjoy the experience. Does the platform have easy-to-access and well-labeled controls? Can someone navigate just using the keyboard? Would live captioning be available or sign language interpreters? Do screen reading apps work with the platform with minimal disruption? If presentations are used, can those be downloaded ahead of time and made readable for hard of sight attendees? Has the agenda been made clear and enough time allotted between sessions to accommodate those who need extra time?

While virtual events and live streaming of in-person events provide a convenient option to those with disabilities, there is still plenty of work to ensure accessibility.

Doing the things listed above makes for a vastly improved experience for those with disabilities, and are also just good practices to adopt in general. By incorporating these practices, you also go the extra mile to increase the inclusiveness of your event and community.

POST EVENT PROCESS

I started Part II of this book walking through the ten steps of launching a community from crafting your values to running the actual event. After going through the sprint to get the community established and to take in the success of wrapping up the first event, what do you do immediately after? While this topic could fall under the "Managing Events" chapter, it is also worth discussing on its own as a bridge, not just to the next event, but also towards building a long-lasting community, which will be discussed more fully in Part III.

Outlined below are some of the more important items to keep in mind as general practices for any event, whether in-person or virtual.

Clean Up

The very first thing after the event is to ensure the venue is returned to its original state. Who is responsible for this will depend on the venue and situation, but this mostly entails storing chairs, rearranging furniture, cleaning up trash, disposing of or wrapping up extra food, and turning off and returning A/V equipment. Even if janitorial or catering staff are responsible for cleaning up, helping is simply the right thing to do and a sign of gratitude to the venue hosts.

For virtual events, the good thing is there is no clean up to worry about. That being said, the rest of the items listed below are still useful steps in wrapping up online events.

After Party

A common thing you may hear is that the real event happens after the event. While, hopefully, the event you just wrapped up was a valuable experience, there is a lot of valuable networking and relationship building that occurs once the event is over. For the Enterprise Sales Forum, there was always a group of a dozen or so attendees lingering after the event, so the group would find a local bar in the area to continue the conversations. As an organizer, it is worth researching a few good bar/ hangout options located nearby, picking one, and making an announcement of the afterparty location during the closing remarks by the MC.

In the online event world, going to a bar or restaurant is not possible, but you can host a virtual afterparty. You can send out a link to attendees before the event concludes for after event networking, either as a group gathering, as virtual cocktail party sessions, or as one-on-one speed networking. Be creative and fun with the ideas and explore different platforms that can enable more engaging online connecting with community members. For the Enterprise Sales Forum, the team uses some of the different event types in Run The World to host networking-related activities after the conclusion of the talk that have gone over well with the community.

Collect Metrics

Metrics help to guide your results over time so your team can make data-driven decisions on ways to improve events. Some useful data includes attendee information (who showed and did not show) from your ticketing or events system, demographics of event attendees to track diversity, and a survey or poll data if that was collected during the event. Some data, such as demographics, may be difficult to obtain because it would need to be gathered from another source. Having this data though goes a long way towards understanding your community and making iterative improvements that enhance engagement and inclusivity. This topic is discussed more in Part III.

Gather Media

The best advertisements for your community are the videos and photos taken from the event. Make sure to collect those media assets soon after the event so they can be made available for attendees and members unable to attend. For virtual events, this is easy to collect, as it would come from the software platform used to host the event. For in-person events, this may come from volunteers and community leaders or from a professional photographer or videographer hired for the event. Once gathered and cleaned up, host the photos and videos online and share the links with the community in the event recap email.

Thank You Notes

A demonstration of gratitude goes a long way, so send a thank you message to the speakers for sharing their time and expertise. Next, thank the venue host and sponsors for their support of the community. Then send a thank you note to all the volunteers who helped during the event. In the chaos of life, it can be easy to miss doing these small things, but they make an impact in building trust and support with the people who have helped the most.

Speaker Honorarium / Gifts

This is a type of payment made for services provided on a voluntary basis. While completely discretionary, a small gift to express gratitude for speakers taking their time to freely participate is a nice show of appreciation. In lieu of money, you can give a gift card of a nominal value or some sort of small gift. For the Enterprise Sales Forum speakers, the gift was a card from the chapter leaders and either a gift card or a customized Enterprise Sales Forum notebook handed out right after the talk or sent online for virtual events.

Team Debrief

Once you have the events metrics collected, at least the data for attendance, it is important to have a team debrief. This gives every member of the team an opportunity to share openly about the event. To keep these debriefs focused, schedule the debrief for 30 minutes and ask of each person the following three questions:

- **What went well during the event?**
- **What could have been better?**

- **How can we improve for the next event?**

Designate someone on the team to take notes and give everyone a chance to share their feedback. Once all feedback has been gathered, evaluate what common themes emerge that could be opportunities to improve on the event experience and assign action items for team members to follow up on those recommendations.

Keep in mind that these sessions are to help the team bond and improve together for the benefit of the community. Therefore, avoid making debriefs a blame session to point out mistakes. Things happen that cannot always be accounted for and sometimes people can just forget a step or two in a process. As a leader, create an environment where everyone feels safe in sharing both the good and bad. Doing so will create a more engaged and enthusiastic team.

Recap Email

The Recap Email is the last part of the event experience and is sent out usually a few days after the event but no later than a week out. This is more than a simple thank you note to attendees; it should be sent to all members of the community (or chapter) so those who could not attend can still get value from the experience. The best recaps sum up the top three or four points made during the event, provide a place to view photos and videos, and include a sign up link to the next event. As with any email, short and sweet is best with just enough to entice attendees to click the link and sign up for the next event.

PART 3 - SUSTAINING THE COMMUNITY

"Success is stumbling from failure to failure with no loss of enthusiasm."

– Winston Churchill

FINDING COMMUNITY MARKET FIT

When you launch your first successful event, it feels like you have won the marathon. After weeks of planning, organizing, promoting, and managing all sorts of details big and small, it is both alleviating and exhilarating to have launched your community and put the first event in the books.

Your first event is only the very beginning of a long journey though. A sobering reality is that most communities fail after a few events because there is no community at all! When I was researching groups on Meetup.com to gain insights into successful communities, I noticed most "communities" only listed about three events before the group went dormant.

The reason is that many of these organizers were fixated *only* on the events. They did not place the community at the center of their vision and did not think long-term; instead, they were hyper-focused on just having a good first event. This is why it is important to always think ahead to the next six events or more, which, as discussed previously, forces you to consider the long-term perspective.

This begs the question, when do you have community? How do you know if the series of events you host is more than just events and becomes a group with shared interests, purpose, and values?

During the first few Enterprise Sales Forum events, it felt more like just running events, albeit of higher quality for salespeople. Events were hosted on the third Tuesday of each month, there was always food and drinks, the topics followed stages of the sales process, and speakers were always compelling and well-prepared. I would notice some of the same people coming month after month, but the numbers were steady on attendance.

By the sixth event, the community was reaching about 100 attendees per event. It was around this time a friend introduced me to a potential speaker. She made the introduction, we had a fascinating first call, and I booked him for the May event as a fireside chat. Normally, I would have gone with another panel talk, but he had such an impressive background and philosophy on sales, a one-on-one interview would be the best format to get his thinking out to the members.

I struggled though, as to how best to promote the talk. No one would recognize his name, so the title I came up with for the event was "Fireside Chat with the First Enterprise Sales Hire by Marc Benioff." It was a mouthful, but the target audience would definitely know Marc Benioff as the founder and CEO of Salesforce.

The event smashed all records for attendance. There were well over 200 attendees, and the team was scrambling, as there were not enough chairs, food, and drinks. The registration desk was barely keeping up. Despite the operational challenges, the talk turned out to be excellent and the feedback was outstanding. The community had hit an inflection point.

Startup entrepreneurs often talk about product market fit. This is when the product finally connects with the core audience and the startup hits their growth curve. For example, a product that gets tens of signups per month now gets thousands. Whereas growth was a challenge before, growth almost happens by itself.

That is what the Enterprise Sales Forum felt like. The community increased membership numbers on the Meetup.com group, and a good number of people would attend, but it was steady. Then growth suddenly took off. Soon after, I remember getting requests to start chapters in other cities. When I asked people how they found out about the community, they would mention the names of people and companies I did not know. Word of mouth had spread beyond just my own professional and social circles.

While it was exciting to see the rapid growth of the Enterprise Sales Forum, it still did not answer the "why" behind reaching community market fit. At an event shortly after the fireside chat, one of the attendees confided her reasons for joining the community. In her words, "I felt isolated at work. It was really lonely, and I did not feel comfortable asking questions. Here, I can ask people questions and they listen and want to help."

More than just hosting great events, a community needs to resonate with people and fill a deeper need. The Enterprise Sales Forum resonated with her because it hit upon her intrinsic need to network and collaborate with others freely so she could become a better sales professional. I heard countless similar stories as I personally spoke with other attendees and read feedback from surveys. It was clear the Enterprise Sales Forum reached its inflection point.

This inflection point is called community market fit. Analogous to product market fit, this is where the community satisfies the needs of the market. In other words, there are enough people who feel the community matches their interests, values, and, most importantly, vision. Reaching community market fit is a critical step in the long-term success of a community.

When the vision of your community aligns with an audience that cares about that vision, you have community market fit.

This is the subtle point about thinking long-term that is important to reiterate. If you focus on events over the vision, you might make the mistake of replicating the one incredibly successful event. This may bring in new people, but it will not create the sticky experience that comes from attendees connecting their motivation and interests with the vision of the community.

When you do reach community market fit, it feels magical. Growth happens without significant effort or engagement by the founders of the community. The community is leading and managing itself, which manifests in several ways:

- Members you do not know take on community leadership roles.
- Volunteers are easier to recruit and their involvement is active and highly engaged.
- People joining the community reach beyond your social network and influence.

- The vast majority of new attendees cite word of mouth as the reason for attending an event.

- Members independently tweet, share, blog, and post content without prompting.

- The bar is continuously raised higher on content quality and the profiles of speakers.

- Member and attendance data trends show a growing cohort of engaged regular attendees.

- Metrics on no-shows, percentage of early event signups, and growth rates trend positively.

This does not mean you are off the hook as a community leader; instead, it means others identify with the passion and vision that started you on your journey. An event-oriented approach without a vision will not develop a groundswell of other people to feel passionate about lending a hand to guide the community. To build the groundswell, you need to create the community flywheel.

THE COMMUNITY FLYWHEEL

The term flywheel may or may not be one with which you are familiar. Mechanical engineers and physicists describe it as a device that provides continuous energy by storing energy it generates through its own momentum. In recent years, it has become a term adopted by business strategists to describe business models that perpetuate themselves to drive continuous growth.

It is also possible to use a similar mechanism to drive continuous growth of a community. By doing the right things from the start, the momentum builds upon itself so that not only does the community grow, but this growth sustains itself for the long-term. This is called the community flywheel.

What puts the community flywheel in motion for event-oriented communities? There are four elements that help establish the flywheel, which I experienced firsthand in expanding the Enterprise Sales Forum:

- **Predictable cycle**
- **High quality**
- **Curated membership**
- **Intrigue & novelty**

The success of the Enterprise Sales Forum depended on earning the trust of sales professionals. The past history of sales meetups was littered with poor experiences ranging from veiled pitches for sales training to recruiting traps. There was often little consistency as to when events would happen, what the topics would be, or who would be speaking. Members commonly shared in their feedback that in comparison with other sales-oriented events, , the Enterprise Sales Forum was much more professionally executed from the management of the event to the quality of content. Some even blocked out the third Tuesday of every month to be sure they could attend the events.

Curation was also a critical component of building trust. Members said meeting other sales professionals like themselves was important. If they were going to give up a few hours of their month to attend a sales-oriented event, members wanted to network with peers and build their professional network. This is what led the community leaders to being more aware of who attended events, signed up as members, and received the newsletter and other promotional notifications.

The fourth element that really drove momentum though was being willing to change the format and content to spark curiosity and interest. Besides the fireside chat with the first enterprise salesperson from Salesforce, the Enterprise Sales Forum team invited VCs and CEOs to speak about sales, let members participate in "Rate My Pitch" events, and brought nationally known speakers in to present. As long as the content was relevant for the audience, these special events created intrigue and buzz as well as brought in different groups that the community had not connected with through the regular events. There was always a spike in membership after hosting these events.

As you think about your own community, give some thought about building trust while keeping things interesting. Consider the cadence of your events and the quality of the content as you build your event schedule. Take extra time to carefully vet and prepare your speakers beforehand. Review the attendee lists to see if you are reaching the right audience. Lastly, be willing to mix things up to build in your own intrigue mechanisms that draw new people into the community.

Once you have the momentum to get your flywheel started, you need to keep it going. This is where the flywheel comes in to take advantage of the energy created in the early stages of your community. There are five steps to creating your community flywheel:

1. Recruiting volunteers to help
2. Building a virtuous promotion cycle

3. Operationalize finance and processes
4. Measuring impact
5. Reinvent and re-energize

Over the next several chapters, I will discuss in more detail each of these steps of the flywheel and how they contribute to building long-lasting and healthy communities. How well you manage each element of the flywheel will impact how stable the community is and the ability to scale if you and your team choose to significantly expand the reach of the community.

Before I dive into the five steps of the flywheel, however, I have to share a cautionary tale and why sticking to the plan is so important.

TRUST THE PROCESS

The boxer Mike Tyson once said something to the effect of, "Everyone has a plan till they get punched in the face." That is not exactly what he said, but the point was clear. When adversity hits, your best laid plans might not mean too much.

This was what launching the Boston Enterprise Sales Forum felt like. I had bold dreams about how Boston could be as large and vital of a community as NYC. Then I got punched in the face a few times. What I learned though was that in times like these, the plan is as important as ever.

Boston made a ton of sense as the next city launch for the Enterprise Sales Forum. It was a reasonable drive from NYC; there were many tech companies growing in downtown, which was a core demographic for the community; and several people reached out specifically about launching a community there. As an added bonus, I already had a few good friends in the area willing to help.

The very first Boston event was a huge success. I repeated the fireside chat format with the Salesforce guy who happened to live in Boston and had become a huge fan of the Enterprise Sales Forum. The second event was almost as successful, getting the support of an up-and-coming Boston startup in the sales enablement technology space. At that stage, I thought I had unlocked the winning formula to scale the forum across the globe.

In planning the third event, I was connected to someone who had built the sales training function from the ground up at HubSpot, a leader in the marketing automation market. They had developed a world class sales organization and I thought it would be amazing to have someone at the very beginning of that journey to share his insights at another fireside chat.

It was the day of the event and as I was driving up to Boston, the pit in my stomach grew larger and larger. There were only twenty signups for the event. Given the typical turnout, that meant anywhere from 15 to 18 people would show. In actuality, only a dozen people were in attendance. My speaker was very gracious though and the content itself was incredibly insightful. However, as I looked at all the empty chairs, I could not help but think I totally messed it up.

The following event was just as poor, but with slightly more people. Conversely, the main issue with that event was the audience; it consisted of mostly random people not in sales, including one person who would blurt out nonsensical questions to the speaker and who I constantly had to cut off. Again, my speaker was gracious and patient, but the embarrassment was tearing apart my confidence.

Was my plan flawed? Did I make some fatal mistakes? Was the Enterprise Sales Forum not ready for prime time? That drive back from Boston was full of questions and few answers.

Instead of scrapping my plans, I decided to double down and execute with more intensity. I found a true local speaker who was the CEO of an outsourced sales lead generation company. I got a better venue through a company that was in the sales enablement market and was helping to support the event. I also tripled the amount of promotion over the previous events. The combination of speaker, support, and promotion helped to turn the tide and netted the Boston chapter over 100 signups, even with an impending snowstorm on the way. Using the same strategy, the following month yielded 100 actual attendees. The Boston Enterprise Sales Forum was becoming an actual community!

Trusting the process is not easy in the face of what looks like epic failure. When I asked other organizers of other communities, they all mentioned "hitting the valley" at some point. That is when, despite all best efforts and intentions, things do not work out for an extended period of time. Any number of issues occur from events with poor attendance and speakers not working out to the mix of attendees being off.

In every instance of hitting the valley, things always turned around and the community came back stronger. Sometimes the valley is just one event, and sometimes it is a few events. It can even take several months. For example, the NY Tech Meetup was just a handful of people for the first few years before eventually becoming a community of over 60,000 members. The core members were committed to the vision of the community and passionate about technology.

I will talk about this later under metrics, but be careful of getting too fixated on numbers. The point is not that 100 people attending an event makes it a success. Rather, focus on execution and the four elements that get the flywheel going. What I did not realize at the time was that some of the people who attended the Boston Enterprise Sales Forum during the "valley" would become the strongest supporters of the community.

Later, when launching the Singapore Enterprise Sales Forum, I focused on execution to get the flywheel going. Even though the number of attendees was not huge, what was building from the first event was a core group that understood the vision of the community and would eventually lead it. I just stuck to consistency, quality, and curating the attendees to get through the valley.

It is hard to rely on the process when you do not see immediate results. However, community building is not about immediate results. That can happen, but the more common journey is a slow build with many valleys interspersed with the peaks. You will have highs and lows, but the process keeps you grounded to your vision so you can allow the community to flourish in its own time.

You only get through the valleys though if you trust the process that led to your initial success. Now, let's build the flywheel!

RECRUITING VOLUNTEERS

I cannot stress enough the critical importance of recruiting co-organizers and volunteers to help lead the community and run events. As you have seen from previous chapters, there are a lot of moving parts and it is easy to miss important steps as the community grows. People will often hear me repeat the following:

ALWAYS BE RECRUITING!

As the founder of the community, you are the catalyst. Even the most dynamic and energetic person cannot do it alone though. It is not really a community if others are not willing to help. So use the outpouring of support for your community to help you create a thriving and healthy community!

As your community grows, you will experience two challenges. First is the ability to maintain focus of your vision, and second is the ability to broadly promote your mission within the local community.

- **Vision** – While your vision is clear, many people introduced to the community still may perceive it as an event or networking group.
- **Promotion** – Community building is a team sport, and growth will only occur if your community is motivated to spread the word.

You address both challenges through the creation of a program to gather volunteers and activate motivated members of your community to get actively involved. Often, people may refer to this as an Ambassador program, but feel free to put your own spin on it. The power of such a program is that it provides your organization the extra reach and bandwidth needed as it grows. More importantly, it empowers your most avid supporters to contribute as valued members of the community.

There is no specific profile that makes an ideal volunteer. Rather, it is an ardent and discernable passion for your vision that matters most. At the core, they must have the heart to help others. Beyond that, a volunteer should be involved in the industry that represents your community and have a personable and welcoming demeanor. In this way, a volunteer is not much different than a founding team member.

As you build your volunteer corps, you will quickly see two kinds of volunteers emerge. Some will eagerly jump in to help and do what you assign them to do. Outside of some initial guidance on how to do a certain task, you do not need to worry much. These volunteers are called doers. Other volunteers will suggest lots and lots of ideas and also seem eager. However, as soon as you assign a task or ask them what they would like to work on, they disappear. These types of volunteers I call talkers.

Be careful when bringing on volunteers that you are getting doers, not talkers. These are people that understand the vision and simply want to help the community because they intrinsically believe the vision. Talkers are destructive to communities. They drain everyone else's time, offer up suggestions that are not aligned with the community, and poison the corps of volunteers you have so carefully recruited to help.

How can you tell a talker from a doer? Assign them a task and observe. Talkers will often not show up, argue about the assignment, or show up and show little focus or enthusiasm for the task. Do not waste time on talkers, avoid them at all cost.

One additional consideration is whether a volunteer has a decent social media presence. This is not necessary, but is a nice to have. Because social media is critical to your promotion efforts, volunteers having an active, professionally-focused social media presence on one or more platforms allows them to be more effective in promotion.

To summarize then what makes a great volunteer:

- Passionate supporter of vision

- Heart to help others
- Currently involved in your industry/ endeavor
- Personable and comfortable socializing
- Doers rather than talkers
- Decent social media presence

Once you have chosen your volunteers, you need to get them involved immediately and leverage their enthusiasm. There are two things every volunteer should do when joining the team. First, volunteers should add their involvement in the community to their professional profile. This can be wherever they are most active socially online, like LinkedIn, Twitter, GitHub, etc. This signals commitment to the community and to their network. In other words, you get promotional lift simply through the multiplier effect of the network, thus generating wider exposure.

Second is to strongly encourage your volunteers to promote the community and events. Considering they volunteered, they are naturally motivated to share. This is easier to do if you include them on your promotion distribution list and send them the Promotion Packet. I discussed this in the "Promotions" chapter, but to reiterate, this is a packet that includes all the email and social sharing information needed for people to share community and event announcements to their networks.

Beyond those first two specific tasks, ask each volunteer how he or she would like to be involved further. There are likely to be many opportunities to become involved, so find ways to leverage the passion and skills of your most engaged members. For example, volunteers can help by managing key tasks at the events, recruiting speakers and sponsors, or contributing to content creation.

Below are some ideas on how to actively involve your volunteers:

- Adding the role of community volunteer to their key social profiles.
- Promoting events through their networks as directed through the Promotion Packet.
- Actively engage content shared through the community social accounts.

- Inviting colleagues to join the community and attend events.
- Attending events on a regular basis and warmly welcoming newcomers.
- Volunteering at events as a greeter, social media contributor, A/V assistant, etc.
- Contributing to content as a blogger, moderator, MC, or event recap writer.
- Introducing community leaders to companies that can host or sponsor.
- Recruiting speakers to join the community for future events and talks.
- Connecting with local influencers and media outlets to help spread the word.

As you build up your team, engage your volunteers often by setting up a regular call or communication with the entire team. You may also want to set up a messaging app like Slack or Whatsapp to make communication more immediate. It is easy for people to lose interest and disappear, especially in a volunteer-driven organization. Give people a reason to stay committed and involved, and do not be concerned with the fear of overcommunication. Most volunteers leave because there was not enough communication.

Pay careful attention to how your volunteers are participating. They should be sharing the community with their network and attending most events. If you see no discernable activity from them over social media, then make sure they are still committed and comfortable sharing with their network. In a similar fashion, if they are not attending events, understand why they are not attending and see if there are other ways they might be able to contribute if regularly attending events is not feasible.

This brings me to the most important aspect of volunteer organizations—understanding motivation. It boils down to connecting to the intrinsic needs within people. One consistent trait in the most engaged volunteers is those who have the "heart to help." They have the right motivation to get involved and have the most successful and enriching experience in a volunteer organization.

There are other motivations, of course, that play a role. The most common ones being:

- Interest in thought leadership
- Learning from others
- Developing one's personal brand
- Meeting like-minded people
- Need for recognition
- Opportunity for business

I mentioned that one of the key tasks of a Community Organizer is recruiting a team. But what you are really doing is drawing in people who love what you do and see your vision. Thus, as opposed to dragging people into your organization that might be initially interested in the moment, you want to cultivate your "true fans."[4]

True fans, in your case, will have the desire to help others to learn and succeed. That is the personal win that resonates in the most engaged volunteers. When you ask potential team members to state their personal "WIIFM" (what's in it for me), listen carefully to what they say and see if a helping heart comes through unprompted. If people are first seeking recognition or business, they will never be a good match. Those people disappear at the first sign of real work. You need to cultivate a community of volunteers that will be loyal to the cause and are doers, rather than talkers.

Your community thrives when you have deployed your true fans to support the cause. Even if those initial volunteers may not have the right skills or aptitude, their passion and energy overcome any shortcomings. The good thing is that most tasks involved in running the community are not difficult, it's the sheer number of things to attend to that requires a volunteer to own and execute upon. You are better off engaging the people around you rather than trying to convince experts to join you. Build up your true fans and you build an unstoppable community!

---

[4] "1,000 True Fans" by Kevin Kelly - https://kk.org/thetechnium/1000-true-fans/

VIRTUOUS PROMOTION CYCLE

In the early days of building your community, promotion feels like a ground and pound strategy. You are hitting all the social networks, sending tons of emails, and telling everyone you know about your awesome community. This is why "Always Be Promoting" is so important; you need to generate awareness when no one knows your community exists or even knows to look for your community.

Once you are a few events in and you are gaining momentum though, you do not need to push so hard to promote. Remember, you are creating a flywheel, so you want to simplify and automate as much as you can to reduce manual and time-consuming effort. You also want to change the motion of your promotion to pull people in instead of pushing them to listen and act.

You only have so much leeway to aggressively promote. In the launch phase, people are willing to give the benefit of the doubt to a founder launching something. After the launch, people are not so forgiving of the endless stream of promotional communications. This goes for the internal communications within the community as well as the external promotions to generate awareness.

The process of communicating in a community requires a balance of persistence and respect. On the one hand, you want to share all of the wonderful things you are doing to advance the vision and to provide great events and content for the community. On the other hand, you also need to recognize that in a noisy and busy world, there is only so much communicating you can do before potentially annoying your members and destroying the trust you have worked so hard to foster.

For communicating externally, it is equally as important to be respectful of the volume of outreach. You do not want to appear to be spammy or needy. It is very easy to lose credibility with people who do not know you, your community, or the reason why you are reaching out to them.

Therefore, how you promote events and grow your membership is critical to get right. You need to get your communications across while respecting the fact that some people are engaged but prefer fewer messages. You want to come across as helpful as opposed to being pushy. If you get the cadence right, you can be ensured of a steady stream of well attended events, strong engagement with content, and a growing member base. Your goal should always be to improve the experience for your members, and that includes how you promote your community.

Your next stage of promotion is to build a virtuous cycle that balances frequency, usefulness, and automation. The goal is to keep the flow of communication steady, make the communication worthwhile and informative, and to do so in a way that minimizes manual effort.

The foundation of a virtuous promotion cycle is built upon four pillars:

- **Dependable communication channel**
- **Building strong advocates**
- **Growing the contact list**
- **Predictable cadence**

Dependable Channel

No matter what anyone says, email is still king when it comes to promoting stuff. All the other channels, like social media, SEM, messaging apps like Slack, etc., are all worthwhile options and might, in your context, works quite well. For example, I have seen very popular Facebook and Whatsapp groups that show heavy engagement. Only email, however, has the simplicity and ubiquity that ensures that everyone can be reached.

For the Enterprise Sales Forum, two types of emails are sent to members. The first is a newsletter email that is global and delivers interesting and insightful content to readers. The second is a transactional-style email to members of a particular chapter with announcements, updates, and recaps of events. There are numerous tools, some of which I share in the Appendix, that can manage the creation, sending, and reporting of emails, as well as help in maintaining them.

One recommendation regarding email is to consider two separate email tools. First, you are covered if there is ever an outage with one tool. Second, newsletter and transactional emails are inherently different. For the Enterprise Sales Forum, I simply used one tool for everything in the beginning for simplicity. Yet a better strategy I found later when scaling is to use a proper email newsletter tool for newsletters, and a simpler tool for transactional, message-oriented emails. Doing so increases deliverability and makes it easier to separate newsletter tasks, which are more customized due to content versus the transactional emails that are easier to automate.

How often should you send out emails? Once a week for a newsletter is about the limit for people's tolerance and to ensure consistent and good open rates. Depending on the content and community, open rates can range from a low of 20% to a high of 60% for newsletters, but over time, newsletter open rates tend to decrease. For transactional emails, four times in one month is the most you ever want to send before recipients unsubscribe.

The other consideration for transactional email that promotes an upcoming event is to make the emails engaging. If your emails are always giving the "PLEASE SIGN UP FOR OUR EVENT" vibe, people will begin to ignore your communications. Try to make event announcement emails more engaging and insightful; perhaps include a short video preview with one of the speakers or a blog post about the upcoming topic. Give people a reason to open your emails.

Can another channel other than email work? On a small scale yes, which is fine if your community will only ever be as big as a few hundred people. As the community scales to many hundreds and thousands, email is still the only channel that has proven to consistently work for outbound messaging to members in a community. However, there are ways to use social media to support and bolster your promotion strategy, something discussed in the "Predictable Cadence" chapter a bit later.

One thing I have not touched on is using email for use to people outside your community. This is a cold email strategy and something I would strongly recommend against. First, you do not have their emails and even if you did, they have not opted into receiving emails, which is a huge no-no in a GDPR world. Even if not for regulatory reasons, using a cold email strategy is an aggressive and spammy method of contacting potential members to join your events and community. Cold email is a push strategy that will alienate your intended audience and sour them from joining in the future. There are much better methods than email for promoting your community to new groups, as discussed below.

Building Advocates

The previous chapter discussed recruiting volunteers. One of the reasons to bring on volunteers is to magnify your promotional outreach. One person sending out a message can only reach so many people, but 10, 50, or 100 people sending out the same message creates exponential reach.

Not everyone wants to or has the time to be a volunteer. Some people have restrictive travel, work, or life schedules. Some people do not have the level of commitment in their heart to get involved. There are also members who believe in the vision of the community and would willingly share something across their network if it did not require much work.

This is what is meant by building advocates. Like volunteers, advocates can help spread the message of the community and promote upcoming events. The only difference is the level of commitment and time involved. These types of lightweight tasks are perfect for those that are supporters, but feel more comfortable supporting the team from the bleachers rather than getting heavily involved on the field.

How do you find advocates? One easy way is to survey members and directly ask if they would be interested in being part of an advocacy team that occasionally shares events and community announcements to their network. Once you have members identified, add them to your Promotion Packet distribution.

As mentioned in the "Promotions" chapter, a Promotion Packet is a document or template with information and announcements you wish to share to the community and beyond. Oftentimes this is for promoting upcoming events, so the packet should include registration links, social media sharing blurbs, images, and other information that assists in promotion.

What an advocacy team enables is a means to accelerate word of mouth marketing. This is by far the best type of marketing because it comes from people who understand the vision, believe in the community, and have their own network of peers where your promotions would resonate. The influence of someone you know holds significantly more sway than an unknown and unwelcome cold email or some website ad that pops up randomly. As word of mouth starts to spread and the community grows, you can add more advocates from the membership base to further scale your promotional reach.

One last idea to broaden reach in an impactful way is to allow volunteers and advocates to publicly identify their support of the community. One way to do this is to add their community involvement as a role on LinkedIn. This allows others in their network to also see the community and their participation, thus conveying trust and credibility onto your community and creating strong social proof.

Growing the List

As you schedule more events, promote over email, and invite volunteers and advocates to share to their networks, you will invariably add more people to your membership, which allows for more email promotion to more people. This is what I mean by growing the list.

Collecting emails is critical as you build your membership base. While other channels may provide better engagement and immediacy, the email is the most scalable way to communicate to all members of your community. Your email list is the most potent and precious asset you possess as a leader.

Given the importance of the email list, it is essential to find one, consistent, and easy to manage way to collect emails. Most email newsletter tools have customizable forms that you can direct people to sign up. These tools will also have GDPR checks and double opt-in flows to ensure your email list is compliant and obeys email list best practices. The sign up form can also be embedded into your website (if you have one) and links within newsletters, transactional emails, and social media.

You can also get more creative with your sign up form. I have added it as a clickable banner in my email signature, sent it out as a social media post, created a QR code for folks to scan to join the community if they were guests at events, and incorporated the link into blog posts for people to sign up. Be inventive and find ways of integrating your sign up form to help build your email list.

There are also other services available for building email lists. Membership SaaS platforms, plug and play membership apps, donation apps, even basic online forms tools can be effective as long as you understand the capabilities and limitations of the solution. The benefit of using a service built for newsletters is the signup flow is integrated into your email platform without having to import/export or synchronize data sources across services.

Of course, not every sign up fits the profile of a member you want in the community. Depending on how open you wish to make your community, you can add more or less fields to your sign up form. Some just ask for an email address to increase the odds of capturing some information; other communities require more information such as name, company, and LinkedIn or other social media profile URL. Just remember that the more information you ask for, the more friction you add, resulting in fewer sign ups.

Once the information is captured, how can you be sure it is accurate and truthful? You could default trust all sign ups and not worry about it. However, as discussed in the chapter on curation, it is important to have a community that members can trust and feel is a true peer-driven network. That trust is the glue that keeps the community thriving. Therefore, it would be worth at least a cursory check to review on the emails being added to your list.

One compromise to maximize sign ups while having enough information to vet people is to ask for an email and one additional piece of information. Most logical would be First (Given) and Last (Family) name, but you might want to ask for Company instead. You could also ask for Name and Company, but then you are starting to risk too much friction.

There are a number of services that can verify emails and names. At a minimum, newsletter platforms usually check emails for validity. You can also turn on double opt-in, and any emails addresses that do not opt-in would be excluded automatically from further communications. The next level would be to leverage contact enrichment tools that will not only verify and clean up data, but also search the Internet for additional information, such as social profiles. These tools can often be plugged into email newsletter platforms to run the verification and enrichment process automatically upon sign up.

There is one last option for verifying email information. For the Enterprise Sales Forum, I hired a virtual assistant from overseas to help in setting up events and managing information across chapters. Given the volume of member data the community had across multiple Meetup.com pages, I asked the assistant to also review and correct or remove member data.

While this was the least automated method, it was also the most accurate. Using human assistance was more important in the early days when I needed greater accuracy in understanding membership demographics. Now all of that work has shifted to automated tools to speed along the process of adding emails to the membership list. While I recommend this hybrid approach in certain situations, you are always better off going with an automated approach if feasible.

Predictable Cadence

Once you have your email list building strategy in place, it is time to put all of these pieces together to build your promotion engine on a predictable cadence. By predictable, I mean establishing a regular frequency, and by cadence, I mean building in automation to execute, track, and measure the results of the promotions so you can iterate and improve.

With frequency, you are delicately balancing awareness versus spam. I discussed email frequency earlier and strongly recommend against anything more than once a week for newsletters and once a week for transactional messages. Most people are very protective of their inboxes and will not welcome frequent intrusions into their work and personal space. While email is king, be conservative with how often you send and question whether you absolutely need to send that email.

For other channels like social media, you want to have a greater frequency because attention spans are even more fleeting. At the same time, you also have to have something interesting or worth sharing besides event updates and self-promotion. Social media is not a one-way channel like email, it works best when you engage.

For frequency over social media, consider content building, posting schedules, and engagement strategies. You need to gather compelling content and slot these into regular intervals. For compelling content, utilize external sources like blogs, videos, podcasts, etc., wherever there are topics relevant to your community. For posting schedules, use an automated social media scheduling tool, many of which are free for lightweight uses (some are mentioned in the Appendix).

Engagement strategies over social media are the one thing you cannot automate. You can set up a schedule where someone from your leadership team will proactively engage over designated social channels and interact on topics that matter to the community. For the Enterprise Sales Forum, some of us would rotate to cover the Twitter account and respond to the sales-related hashtags or interact with sales influencers.

When engagement time is scheduled, your social channels do not feel like one-way, broadcast only channels. There are too many social spaces set up by communities that seem abandoned and feel like online ghost towns. Your social presence should be as lively as your community events, which is how you will build an audience that is drawn to your community.

One thing that will help regarding social media engagement is limiting the channels you use. The rule of thumb should be to hang out online where your community hangs out. For salespeople, that is most likely LinkedIn.

For developers, they are more often on Twitter. Find where your community is and set up shop there.

Between email tools and a social media scheduling tool, you should be able to keep steady track of your cadence. At least from an execution and tracking standpoint, you can build up content ahead of time, have it locked and loaded through your various tools, and spend time on more immediate matters such as event scheduling, managing community matters, and creating great content.

What about measuring, iterating, and improving? Most of the free tools have limited analytics, mostly because vendors want customers to pay for their software. Email is generally pretty easy to track, as any tools will, at a minimum, provide open and click through rates. Social media can be more difficult, though you can use the Advertising tools provided by Facebook, Twitter, and Instagram to pull engagement metrics such as views, likes, and shares. The only downside is none of these sources can be aggregated, so you will have to manually bring the data together using a spreadsheet or dashboarding tool.

Remember that cadence involves two strategies. The first is expectation setting with existing members regarding communications. The second is a long-tail strategy to build awareness and gain new members. Over time, people will share your emails, follow your social media accounts, and may even be compelled to share or respond to postings. The long tail strategy only works if you have a cadence, share relevant content, and regularly engage across social channels.

OPERATIONALIZE & REPEAT

When you are initially building a community, managing finances, and building operational rigor are not high priorities. Just the initial work to get the community launched, to promote and run events, and to grow your membership are all consuming. Without established practices to manage money and processes however, it will be difficult to grow your community.

In the early days, managing finances will mostly mean tracking expenses. This might include software fees, name tags and pens, catering, venue fees, transportation costs, etc. Whatever the fees, make sure to clearly categorize the expenses and save the receipts. It is suggested to get an app to scan receipts and capture relevant details digitally so you can have one place to report from when tracking expenses and reporting taxes (if required).

Once you begin monetization, you will also need to track revenue from members. Most event platforms already record ticket sales and will report on year-end earnings minus their fees (make sure to record these fees as expenses). The same applies to charging membership fees, though that might be in a separate app if you use other software for managing memberships.

Should you bring on sponsors, you will need a way to bill them. Depending on the company and their processes, you might just need a method to take credit card payments. There are a number of payment apps and gateways that you can use that charge a nominal fee depending on region. There are also an increasing number of accounting packages that enable credit card payments. If credit card payments are not allowed or an invoice needs to be generated, accounting packages can easily handle this functionality and there are many high-quality, free, or low-cost SaaS tools available (check in the Appendix).

Managing operations and processes should be done centrally using an online office suite. Which you choose comes down to personal preferences. For the Enterprise Sales Forum, I decided on Google for setting up an email account, office suite, and online cloud storage location. Microsoft is also a viable option with their Office 365 suite and cloud storage. Regardless of choice, a separate and shared email account will ensure various tools used are not tied to an individual organizer in the event that organizer leaves or is not available. Using an online office suite allows everyone to share and collaborate on files from one place like docs and spreadsheets and presentations. With cloud storage, you can upload and download files internally with the organizing team and externally to members, which is especially helpful when capturing photos and videos from events.

For quick communications and messaging, either Slack or a Whatsapp group are useful to keep the team connected. You may have better alternatives or platforms more appropriate for your region that are preferred, though. The benefit of having a dedicated communication channel is the team can be in continuous communication about updates, changes, and emergencies.

As the team grows and changes, having a way to manage and track who is doing what becomes more important. I have found that a simple workflow visualization tool can be helpful to keeping people on the same page and tracking progress towards deadlines. Any number of tools can work (and are free for small teams). A tool that works well on mobile devices is preferred because alerts are more effective on the device people most have available to them and can quickly refer to during team meetings.

On the topic of meetings, during the initial stages of community building and event planning, a cadence of every few days makes sense. These do not have to be long meetings, but it helps to keep the team coordinated and also helps in building trust and rapport. If you have messaging and work/project management tools setup, then you do not have to arrange as many meetings, but never lose sight of the fact that community organizing is a people-oriented effort. The people are always more important than the tools.

Lastly, you should consider creating an Operations Guide. This guide lays out how you specifically run the community and the tools and processes to manage the community. It should not be too long, since you want to make sure new people on the team read it and it becomes a living guide for the team to capture changes as the community changes.

You may wonder then if this book was the operations guide for the Enterprise Sales Forum. Yes and no. You would be correct that much of the content here started from the first operations guide I created. As I was establishing local chapters across the globe, I needed one document to explain how to launch a chapter from scratch. However, that guide was only a fraction of the size because what goes into the operations guide is purely focused on running events. Eventually, I condensed the guide down further into a four page checklist!

The event checklist has been an incredibly useful tool for the Enterprise Sales Forum in order to track what is and is not done. In a meeting, the checklist can guide where things stand, what roadblocks exist, and what needs to be expedited. A checklist is also very visual and easy to share online, so the entire organizing team can be continuously up to speed on planning for an event. I share two checklists that have been used by the Enterprise Sales Forum in the Appendix to help guide your checklist creation.

With any process, guide, or checklist, keep in mind the acronym KISS, or "Keep It Simple, Stupid." Lots of rules and convoluted processes can easily discourage folks from participating and being creative. There is value in rigor because it makes things repeatable, but at the same time, spontaneity can unleash innovation and new opportunities not yet explored.

In the vain of keeping it simple, this chapter is pretty short for a reason. Decisions on whether to set up a legal entity, what type of entity, how to manage finances, who handles the bank account, how to handle taxes, what type of insurance you need, etc., all are very much regional or country-based. Refer to the Appendix on thoughts on creating a legal entity, and reach out to local resources and information for guidance to questions regarding company formation, taxes, and regulations.

MEASURING IMPACT

The ability to measure what you do allows you to understand where and how to improve. Without that understanding, decision-making is based more on opinions and whim rather than on reality. The subtle point here is knowing what specifically to measure so your "where to improve" results in affecting meaningful outcomes that sustain and grow the community.

It is important to emphasis this point right away:

Having a large number of members is not the success criteria. Success is in the growth of value created within and by the community.

The mistake that is often made by most community builders is in using signups or memberships as proxies of community health. Signups are absolutely not a useful metric to assess the strength of a community. In fact, obsessing over the aggregate number of people in your community can actually lead to a false sense of security that obscures warning signs about your community.

I made this very same mistake with the Enterprise Sales Forum in the beginning. As I was launching chapters, I was also struggling to understand what would lead to sustainable communities. After all, going through the effort to build chapters just to have them fold would be a huge waste.

This was where the "true fans" post mentioned earlier in the "Recruiting Volunteers" chapter provided some insight. If each chapter built up to 1,000 members and 10% of that group would attend events any given month, that would lead to a strong monthly showing of 100 people to create excitement around the event and create a self-sustaining flywheel through word of mouth.

The mistake I made was on two fronts. First, I was caught up in every chapter needing to reach 1,000 members as a litmus test for community health. Second, I assumed each event needed 100 people to generate excitement.

Getting to 1,000 members is incredibly difficult. It was easy in NYC to build to 1,000 people because it is a city of over 8 million and a metropolitan area of over 20 million people. It also happened to have a thriving meetup culture, a rising tech startup ecosystem, and lots of younger professionals willing to spend their evening at an event. Many other cities did not have that same culture or the sheer population to attract 1,000 B2B enterprise salespeople.

As the community hosted more and more events, I started to see the value in smaller groups. Enterprise Sales Forum events felt comfortable at 75 attendees, but there were also events with 20 people that were amazing, such as the Sales Manager Roundtables or talks with 35 people in places like Singapore and Hong Kong that formed tight-knit communities.

What I came to understand was that absolute size meant less than magnitude of impact. Things tend to be easier at a certain scale, like in promotions and recruiting. The success and long-term viability of a community does not require lots of people though. Success comes from the strength of the alignment to the vision. For that alignment to take hold, it requires as few as a handful of people.

There is a theory in social networking called the "90-9-1 Rule." It states that for any community built around a network, 90% will be lurkers, 9% will be engaged, and 1% will be heavily involved super users. Specific numbers are less important though than the magnitudes they represent. For communities built around in-person events, these numbers can look like 70-25-5 or 60-30-10. Every community has sporadically engaged lurkers, but what is important is the "engaged" and "super users" are involved and feel motivated by the vision of the community.

So how does any of this relate to measuring impact? Another theory in the social networking world often cited is "Metcalfe's Law." The basic premise is that the more people in a network, the greater the value for everyone in the network. Therefore, based on the theory, more value is created from 100 people than from 10. This is what powers Facebook, LinkedIn, Twitter, and other social networks.

Determining what to measure then becomes an exercise in understanding the impact of the community to create and foster that value. This goes back to the earlier discussion about vision and values. Success is in how that value in the community grows. Therefore, measurement requires understanding the value members receive from the community and how they weigh those values.

The community can be evaluated along three key metrics that enable organizers to evaluate and take actions that support the health of the community:

- Level of satisfaction of benefits community members receive
- Weighting of the importance of those benefits
- Likelihood of recommending the community to their network

I call these community pulse metrics, as they speak most directly to the attitudes and feelings of members. The value of these metrics is they give the most unvarnished and transparent view of both the experience and quality of community. Just as an EKG gives doctors an indicator of a patient's health, community pulse metrics do the same for community organizers.

It is worth mentioning the terminology switch from value to benefit in the metrics above. The term "benefits" is used for the sake of clarity when surveying and asking questions of the community. The world "value" can seem vague, but benefits speak more closely to tangible features that directly relate to how members and non-members experience the community.

Before I dive into each one of the community metrics, there are four other types of data and metrics worth gathering: demographics, diversity, engagement, and growth.

- **Demographics** – This is census data of your community such as the roles, skills, seniority, or industry, whatever is necessary to get an understanding of make-up of the community. The other thing to monitor is the change in demographics over time, which can provide insights into how promotions and content are impacting who is drawn to the events and community. Capturing this information is important when seeking financial support since organizations will ask for these statistics in making sponsorship decisions.

- **Diversity** – While this would normally be included as demographic data, it is becoming even more important to show the gender and racial composition of communities. This demonstrates the seriousness of a community's commitment to diversity and inclusion efforts and can provide guidance into improving diversity of the membership.

- **Engagement** – These are measures of how involved people are with the community, events, and promotions. Consider measures such as attendance versus no-show rates, the percentage of repeat attendees, and interactions over email and social media like opens, clicks, and shares. Along with community pulse metrics, engagement metrics give insights into how participants feel about the experience and content. Information such as repeat attendees is particularly valuable, as that is the 9% and 1% layers of your community that will draw in volunteers and leaders.

- **Growth** – These metrics cover how the community scales over time. These are the top line numbers like number of members in the community over time, growth in attendance across events, number of social media followers, and size of the email list. These are useful data, but not the most important. Because these are the easiest to see and collect, the tendency is to focus on these numbers rather than the other metrics. Another thing to keep in mind is that growth metrics are only valuable over an extended period of time, given the number of unpredictable variables between events and over shorter timeframes.

Yet, of all the types of metrics described above, the ones that most matter in ensuring community continuity and growth are the community pulse metrics. Below is a more thorough explanation of each metric and why it is important.

- **Satisfaction of Benefits** – Hopefully, you know how your community benefits members. If you are unsure, write down what you think the advantages are and then interview a few of your most avid members. Then you can survey the entire community to evaluate how satisfied they are with the delivery of those benefits by the community. In essence, you are asking if the community fulfills the goals that the events and community promises to attendees and members. These benefits will depend on what matters most for your community, but some ideas include:
  - **Networking and meeting peers**
  - **Innovation and learning**
  - **Quality of content (speakers, topics, newsletter, etc.)**
  - **Event experience (venue, technology, etc.)**
  - **Community (inclusiveness, helpfulness, safety, etc.)**
- **Relative Value of Benefits** – This is more of a weighing metrics to determine which of the benefits are important in the eyes of the community. Knowing this allows the community to better tailor the content and experience to what the community says they want (and by extension, do less of the things they do not care about as much).
- **Recommend the Community** – If you have ever been involved in customer success or support roles, you would recognize the last question as similar to an NPS, or Net Promoter Score, metric. This is measured on a scale from 1 to 10 with a 9 or 10 being a promoter of the product or service. In this case, I am adapting it for the purposes of understanding community loyalty and experience.

One additional metric you may want to include is an overall satisfaction score of the entire community. Based on the community, there may be value in having a holistic number that sums up the overall impressions of the community experience. It is entirely optional, though.

How do you capture these metrics? Demographic, diversity, engagement, and growth are all available through the tools you use to manage the community. For community pulse metrics, that requires a survey tool. If in-person, you can use paper and pen surveys, but a more modern method is to have members scan a QR code to open an online survey tool and take the survey towards the end of the event. You can even do a raffle to encourage participation.

There are numerous survey technologies to use, even free form builder tools, and any will suffice for these simple surveys. Aim to create surveys that can be completed in less than two minutes, any longer will risk losing respondents. Simplicity and brevity will ensure you get a high response rate and give you more data to work with for analyses. However you set up your surveys, make sure you leave at least one free form textbox to collect longer thoughts from members.

There is an affliction known in some communities called death by survey. Be careful of doing so many surveys that it turns off members. A good rule of thumb is one survey during the end of each event to capture immediate feedback and then a more comprehensive survey sent out once per quarter for bigger questions you may have or to float possible changes.

Sometimes there is a question whether to publish the results publicly. This question often comes up when the results show that the members are disappointed in some aspect of the community. You are better off sharing the results openly with the community however and adopting a culture of complete transparency. It is after all a community and without trust, even in light of negative comments or discontent, it will be very difficult to build a thriving and productive community.

There is a lot here to consider on the topic of metrics, but know that you do not have to collect everything all at once. Give yourself time to build the metrics habit among the leadership team, and focus on a few important metrics that can guide your efforts early on. Then over time, you can build in more metrics and create dashboards to provide a holistic view of community health to everyone.

How do you make decisions based on the data you see though? That is what I tackle next.

REINVENT AND RE-ENERGIZE

Launching a community in many ways resembles launching a startup. There are many more unknowns than certainties, there are never enough resources, and getting to market fit is a winding journey. The other way communities and startups are similar is they both are continuously iterating towards a repeatable and scalable model.

Steve Blank, the tech startup entrepreneur and godfather of the lean startup movement, coined this definition of startups over a decade ago. It also applies to what it takes to build a community from the ground up. You are experimenting, testing, learning, and implementing on a continuous basis so you can reach a repeatable and scalable community. In other words, building the community flywheel.

The last part of flywheel is perhaps the most important of the steps. Many communities suffer from a disease called same-itis. This is where every event is the same template repeated over and over again without variation. While there is some value in a repeatable and dependable model, in time your members start to grow bored with the lack of spontaneity. As mentioned when discussing the flywheel, part of what keeps members engaged is building novelty into the content and experience.

This is what is meant in this chapter by reinvent and re-energize. Community leaders should always be on the lookout for different ways to engage their members and bring novel experiences and content that both excite current members and entice new people to attend.

Another common startup concept is "Failing Fast." This is how startups can iterate so quickly, enabling smaller, less resource-rich teams to outpace better equipped incumbents. Though community is not a "competitive market," you are competing for the time and attention of a fickle audience that has many choices of how they wish to spend their time. The way communities stay nimble and innovate then is to come up with new ideas, try them out, and drop the failed ideas while keeping the good ones.

How do you choose what new ideas to pursue? This is where surveys help. Not only do surveys give guidance from members on what is working and not working, but the free form text boxes suggested in the previous section also provide a wealth of unfiltered opinions and valuable ideas. New ideas can also come from other communities, content from blogs, or simply your own musings. There is no formula for innovation, just a willingness to experiment, being transparent with the community, and having the discipline to measure and assess outcomes truthfully. That is how to fail fast in the community context.

One of the experiments I ran at the Enterprise Sales Forum was a program to improve the diversity of the community. I noticed attendance for some events was over 90% men. I was wary of doing just another "Women in Sales" event, though, to drive more women attendees. I knew to have a lasting impact on changing the ratio I would have to consider multiple events and build excitement around the event. So instead of a Women in Sales event, I launched Women in Sales Month for all of October.

The premise was simple. All chapters would host a panel discussion with all women sales leaders during the month of October under the banner of Women in Sales month. The topic could be anything sales related, but the promotion would be "WOMEN IN SALES" for every October event.

The results were outstanding! Events for that month registered over 50% women attendees and the number of women signing up to the community grew appreciably. Now, October is a month reserved by the Enterprise Sales Forum for Women in Sales and recognized by other sales communities as well.

On the other hand, not all experiments work. The Enterprise Sales Forum forged a partnership with a sales training technology startup. The idea was to provide access to their sales training content for free to anyone in the community as a way for the startup to get paid corporate sign ups. After one month of promotion, no one signed up. The team quietly ended the promotion and moved onto other programs.

The lesson here is that being nimble and flexible pays dividends. Not every experiment will yield positive results, but that is to be expected. When presented imperfect data and tight timelines, which is the case for community building, the most informed guess will usually suffice. That is because even a failed experiment is an opportunity to learn and another step towards getting to successful outcomes.

The spirit of experimentation and innovation is what also makes the community fun and interesting for organizers and volunteers. Depending on the cadence of your events, you might consider brainstorming sessions on a bi-monthly or quarterly basis with the team to come up with new ideas, improvements to processes, and ways to better engage the community. Doing so sends a message that innovation is welcome and those most involved have a say in guiding the future of the community.

This finalizes the five parts of the community flywheel. Starting from the beginning, you want to recruit volunteers, build the promotion engine, operationalize and automate, measure what is most important for members, and foster innovation to keep the community engaged. Do these things well and you will create a feedback loop that brings in more volunteers, powers your promotion, and enables better ways of operating. Then measuring results give you insights into experiments that work versus ones that do not add value. That is the foundation of a long-lived and healthy community.

DEALING WITH SETBACKS

Building a community can often feel like taking two steps forward and one step back. I shared some of the inevitable calamities you will face in the introduction and you will also face your own challenges and mistakes along the way. The point to always keep in mind is that even when you get hit by setbacks, you are still making progress.

Elon Musk, famous tech entrepreneur and founder of both Tesla and SpaceX, once said, "Running a startup is like chewing glass and staring into the abyss." That is because of all the unknowns involved and dizzying ups and downs that constantly leave startup founders spinning. In a similar way, building a community resembles the startup journey with you in the role of community entrepreneur.

Up to this point, I have shared mostly the positives about community building. I have also encountered my fair share of problems and conflicts and full-scale screw-ups. I am pretty sure I have many more mistakes left to make along the way. No matter the situation, however, the Enterprise Sales Forum always found a way to overcome, a testimony to the right team doing enough of the right things, and being humble enough to own mistakes and learn from them.

Below are some of the challenges you might face. I saw all of these with the Enterprise Sales Forum and other communities I have built or helped to build. Hopefully, by knowing these upfront, you can avoid or mitigate the worst of these situations.

Cult of Personality

A founder of a community has a huge influence over community dynamics. In the early days, this is helpful and gives a face to the community. As one person dominates the community long-term however, it can hinder growth. The community perceives the leader is more interested in fame and attention which disincentivizes others to take on volunteer and leadership roles. Even though a founder does not want to create a cult of personality, that can happen inadvertently if not careful.

To prevent this, always remember that community is about vision over people. Community only grows into a self-sustaining entity when the founder(s) do not matter as much anymore. The founders and history are fine to remember, but it is critical to give space for other leaders to come up the ranks and bring their own ideas into the organizations, which is discussed later in this chapter.

The best way to mitigate against the "cult of personality" is to have a team of leaders so one person does not overly dominate. Rotating overall leadership of the community also helps to disperse the influence of one person and lets the community know that anyone is welcome to be a leader.

Bureaucracy

One of the things that happens to all organizations as they scale is more people become involved in decision making. This can be good because it brings more perspective and brainpower. The downside is getting caught in the analysis paralysis where the team gets stuck on solving a problem.

You need a better way to make decisions. In those instances when decision making stalls, ask yourself what is the best thing that could happen and the worst thing that could happen. Chances are good that the worst thing is not so terrible, and the best thing is promising. In other words, give yourself a chance to take on some risk when managing your community. The community values and a culture of transparency will go a long way in making sure your decisions as a leader stay true to the spirit of the community.

The other aspect about bureaucracy that occurs is compartmentalization. This is when people or teams only focus on their team and ignore the work of other teams. You can prevent this by having open communication channels like regular team meetings and online chat. Keeping the leadership team small also keeps compartmentalization at bay. Once a team starts to get to over eight leaders, things can become unwieldy and decision making slows. Guidance was provided on an optimal team format in the "Building a Team" chapter.

People and Personalities

There will no doubt be issues that arise with people not getting along. Personalities will clash and things may be said that cause strife. As a leader, it is important to be aware of these issues, especially in the leadership and volunteer teams. Even minor grievances can cause major headaches later on and create collateral damage, which lowers moral and causes people to take sides.

The time to act is before there are consequences, so take a proactive approach. The best thing is to talk things out among the people with grievances. Never take a side, but listen and encourage each person to also listen to those with whom they disagree. Oftentimes, just the act of listening and setting the stage for a blameless conversation can heal wounds and build trust.

Turnover in Leadership

There will be the inevitable changing of the guard as some leaders step down. This can happen because of work or life changes, more travel, or simply a desire to move on. While it can be disruptive when a fellow leader leaves, it should not be seen as a negative. Leaders stepping down is to be expected and everyone that does resign should be warmly thanked for their contributions.

Leadership turnover in communities tends to be quite high; therefore, having a succession plan and roster of potential leaders to backfill should be a key task before the community reaches one year of existence. The best pool of leader candidates will be from the volunteer ranks.

The best prospective leaders exhibit most of the traits outlined for volunteers, but show strength in two particular areas. First, they are extreme doers. They do not need to be told what to do, they act when they see something that needs doing, and get it done. They possess "bias for action" in spades. Second, they are a vocal believer of the vision. They proudly raise the flag of the community and actively talk about and promote it to others.

Personal Burnout

The biggest reason most leaders and volunteers stop contributing actively is burnout. To give yourself freely to anything for an extended period of time can be challenging. That is especially the case when it comes to community that can be draining with all the ups and downs.

There have been plenty of times I have experienced burnout and it can take weeks or even months to recover. The stress, anxiety, disappointment, fear, and loneliness are tightly wound up in your mind, and it takes time to unscramble that toxic mess.

You might think loneliness is an odd emotion to feel in a community with lots of people. More often than not, organizers are not gregarious or outgoing personalities. There is also the pressure to maintain a positive demeanor in front of the community, so a lot of raw emotions are repressed. Many organizers have no reliable outlet to spill their guts and, therefore, feel trapped.

This is why trusting the community leadership team is so critical to establish from the beginning. With trust comes open and transparent sharing of both the good and the bad. The best way to defeat burnout is to be open about the stresses and being honest with yourself when you need to step away for a break. The leadership team is a team after all, so give members of the team the option to take breaks.

Diversity and Inclusion

While discussed earlier in the "Curating Membership" chapter, it is important to reiterate the importance of incorporating diversity and inclusion at the start. The biggest failure of organizers is to wait too long on addressing this aspect of community. The result is that it is much harder to turn the tide and build an inclusive culture.

The best way to ensure diversity and inclusion is part of the community's foundation is to bring diverse voices to the leadership team. While this may be very difficult to do early on, if the founding team is diverse, then diversity will be seen as important by the community and folded into how you think about content, speakers, promotions, and sponsorships.

If you cannot build diversity into the team from the beginning, plan to grow diversity in the volunteer base. Seek out people in other similar communities that are influencers in diversity and inclusion to help amplify the call for volunteers. Also, call out the need for volunteers representing diverse backgrounds in your promotional materials and during the events; if you repeat the message enough, the community will respond to help.

Member Safety

Whenever you get a bunch of random humans together, there is bound to be some friction that arises between people. Despite the best intentions of the community and the diligence of the organizers, there are the rare occasions that someone steps out of bounds in a way that offends, harasses, or threatens members of the community.

This is why communities enact a Code of Conduct (CoC). This is discussed more in the Appendix, as there are many changing perspectives on how to develop a CoC. The key point is that a CoC clearly lays out what is out of bounds from a behavior and speech perspective and the policies to address violations.

It is important to emphasize that trust is the bedrock on which community is built upon. Therefore, with any CoC violation, community leaders must be as transparent as possible with enforcement actions to the extent that does not create further harm. If trust is broken in the community, psychological safety disappears, and members start to abandon the community en masse.

Should a situation ever escalate to threatening or violent behaviors, do not hesitate to call the local authorities. They are more equipped to deescalate or detain individuals so that you and the team can restore the sense of peace and safety in the community.

The other type of safety issue worth mentioning is regarding health situations during events. There may be times when someone falls ill or has an accident requiring medical assistance. In these situations, seek immediate medical attention from trained professionals. The details of the incident and responsibility can be sorted out afterwards once the person is stabilized. As a community leader, the safety of members needs to be on top of your list of things to keep in mind.

Financial Stress

While many communities can exist without much funding or revenue, there is still some nominal amount that is needed to keep the community afloat. That money can go towards software fees, equipment costs, professional services, food and beverage (if not sponsored), and a myriad of other costs that build up over time.

On the revenue side, most communities will monetize either through event fees, sponsorships, or membership fees. Usually the revenue can more than cover the nominal costs of managing the community. Situations can arise, though, when revenue dries up for an extended period of time, such as if you could not host in-person events, sponsors leave, or members refuse to pay fees.

When budgeting, create three budgets in a spreadsheet. One consists of revenues at the maximum based on prior data; the second is the median budget that presumes only modest revenue gain. Finally, the third is the doomsday budget where revenue goes to zero. Then you can build multiple scenarios to prioritize, reduce, or eliminate spending so that even in the most dire of situations, the community could still function.

If the gap is still vast, find ways to substitute for lower cost tools and services. On the revenue side, brainstorm creative ways to bring in sponsors. As an example, to help fund one of the Enterprise Sales Forum chapters, the organizers hosted a recruiting event and sold table space. As a last ditch effort, you can also reach out to your members about the situation and launch a funding campaign using some of the popular crowdfunding services.

Data Privacy and Sharing

When people sign up to events and join the community, what is done with the data that is collected? This is an important consideration because any breach in the trust with how that data is handled can easily destroy the hard earned trust and credibility of the community.

I recommend having a blanket policy of never sharing member data with third parties, even with sponsors and venue hosts. This can cause consternation with organizations financially supporting your community. It is important to never give into these demands because doing so opens your community up to accusations of dishonesty and self-dealing.

The recommended approach to handling these requests is to allow sponsors and the venue host to collect business cards or information at the event. This could be at a dedicated table staffed by the sponsor, at the registration desk with a bowl and sign from the sponsor to collect cards, or through a survey the sponsors shares during the event. It is even better to have sponsor representatives attend the event to mingle with attendees in-person or through online networking time to mutually share information.

There may be times that arise when information gets mishandled or the community gets accused of sharing contact information. The Enterprise Sales Forum faced this issue when a salesperson cold emailed members claiming to be a sponsor. The company was not a sponsor, but it caused all sorts of headaches for the chapter team. It turned out the salesperson merely scraped the Meetup.com members page for that chapter and used a sales email tool to automatically figure out the email addresses for the members.

The lesson is to always be transparent as a community leader and never enter any arrangement that involves sharing member data. If a breach does happen, apologize, and explain the situation with remedies taken to ensure future breaches are avoided. If it is malfeasance, ban the person or company involved and communicate the issue with the community.

How then to deal with sponsors and venue hosts that insist they are entitled to contact data? Explain that protecting member data is a core value of the community and that any such arrangement would, in the long-run, irrevocably damage the community. Most will relent if you explain the importance of trust among the community and that sharing contact data will only harm the community the sponsor is trying to support.

Acts of Nature

In legal contracts, you will often see the term "force majeure," which means contractual obligations and liabilities are cancelled due to an extraordinary event or circumstance beyond the control of the parties. It is basically an admission that all bets are off in light of overwhelmingly difficult events like natural disasters, war, epidemics, etc.

There will be times when these circumstances affect an event. In those cases, there is usually the option to reschedule or to put a temporary pause on events until the timing is more ideal. But what if a global phenomenon shuts down all events and puts the economy on pause?

The year 2020 saw the first such incident as a pandemic made all in-person events impossible to host for months. Everything went fully virtual, even large scale conferences that cost millions of dollars to produce and bring attendees and speakers from all across the world.

Humility and help are two pillars to guide you and the community during these times. The attention during difficult times needs to be on healing, recovery, and support. The last things on anyone's mind are events and community. The only community that matters is the community of first responders working tirelessly to save lives and help those in need.

Humility in the context of community means acknowledging the situation and communicating that to members in a sincere way. The second part is to offer help in a meaningful and heartfelt way. Then you step away and let time pass for the situation to stabilize.

What is normal may look very different from the normal prior to the act of nature. For COVID-19, this meant having to rethink the in-person as a virtual experience. Many communities, like small meetups, simply put an indefinite pause on activities. The Enterprise Sales Forum went fully virtual, hosting talks on platforms like Zoom and Run The World. The pandemic forced the leadership team to scramble, think creatively, and execute a different plan. Being nimble, however, made it easy to make the switch.

Reading through this list of setbacks might appear daunting and scary. Do not be alarmed though. You will inevitably run into challenges along the community journey. Embrace the mishaps, keep an open mind, and you shall overcome!

SUSTAIN VERSUS SCALE

At some point, as your community thrives and reaches a point of stability and consistency, the question of growth will come up. Do you want to be a modest-sized community, or do you want to take the leap and build a larger organization that is national or even global? My answer to that is:

Scale is optional!

It is important to define scale as a difference in magnitude in growth rather than being another word used for growth. Growth can be modest in change and size, or it can be exponential. Scale is a purposeful effort to expand an organization at a significantly faster growth curve. Growth is simply a way of iterating and evolving as a healthy organization. The type of growth that is more modest and not focused on size is called sustaining growth.

Do not think of sustaining growth as stagnation or no growth. As shared in an earlier chapter, healthy communities find ways to keep members engaged and involved. Without things that attract new members, the group grows stale, people leave, and you have fewer new people engaged. This is the slow spiral of death that causes many successful communities to calcify and eventually shut down.

Therefore, growth is not optional. Growth is the life of any community. What is optional is the choice to scale. There are three types of scale to consider: geographical, horizontal, and online.

Scaling geography is growing across physical regions. That could mean across different cities or states, or can mean going across countries. This type of scaling can seem like a wild and chaotic ride. It stretches the capabilities of the team, opens up incredible opportunities and crushing defeats, and can feel at times that the entire community is going to implode. This type of scale is incredibly taxing on resources and time. There is setting up of chapters, training new chapter leaders, and preparing for a successful launch. Once new chapters are launched, it is just as challenging to keep all the chapters connected and aligned to the vision. This type of scale requires a lot of communication and a ton of trust.

Scaling horizontal is to grow into additional knowledge areas or professional domains. In essence, it is creating communities that care about different, yet closely related, topics. This is opposed to scaling vertically, as above, which would be to grow the size of the community in only one topic area. This tends to be the easiest way to scale since it does not require setting up in different locations and the topics are related. As an example, you could have a community for digital marketers and then expand into growth marketing. The Enterprise Sales Forum did something similar, creating the Sales Development Forum to serve salespeople just starting their careers in sales.

Scaling online is taking the in-person experience and making it available in a virtual space. For example, some communities have added forums or messaging apps as an online option for people to connect, share, and network between in-person events. Some communities also opt to use the group features of the major social networks, or pay for software specifically built to support communities as a platform.

Online scaling has become the most common way to scale a community in 2020 as the pandemic swept the globe. It is a very different type of medium to master. Many attempts suffer from the empty party problem in which there is not enough participation or experience the signal versus noise problem in which too many people are posting without guidance or direction. The benefits of getting online scaling correct are enormous since online provides access to people around the world.

If you do decide to expand, revisit your "why" as well as your values and your own level of commitment and availability. Launching the Enterprise Sales Forum nationally and then globally was an all-consuming experience that required total commitment. Anything less would have resulted in a poor experience for members, chapter leaders, and speakers. Furthermore, it would have tarnished the reputation of the organization in the eyes of those who I most wanted for the community. Therefore, make sure the leadership agrees and is committed to the mission!

PART 4 - PARTING THOUGHTS

"If we can fall in love with serving people, creating value, solving problems, building valuable connections and doing work that matters, it makes it far more likely we're going to do important work."

— Seth Godin

CONCLUSION

After reading this far, have I put you off to the thought of building a community? I certainly hope not! It is an uncertain and bumpy journey, but realize you can indeed pull this off. You CAN start a vibrant and engaging community while having a positive impact on the lives of many people. But it requires you to roll up your sleeves and do a lot of the heavy lifting at the start.

If there is one lesson I want you to take from this book it is you do not have to do this alone. You have the passion, so use that passion to inspire others to join the cause. The heavy lifting becomes more manageable and even a pleasant task when shared with others who are equally enthusiastic. Be as much of a team builder as you are a community builder.

If there is room for a second lesson, it's that community is not about size and scale. What is important is the impact to the lives of the people the community touches. What the community builder cares most about is building passion around those shared values and interests. When a community forms around an interest, the combined human potential that is brought together has the power to impart a lasting change in the world and shape the future of those in the community for the better.

The last parting thought I want to share is that you have to love what you do, with an important caveat. In the book The Radical Leap by Steve Farber, it reads:

Do what you love in the service of those who love what you do.

You do not build a community in a vacuum. You build it to connect others in the hope they value not only the community, but also those working to make the community possible. That is the ultimate flywheel, the cycle of reciprocal appreciation that builds upon itself. Even in times when I was at my most stressed and exhausted, hearing the positive words from members of the community helped me carry on. Love what you do, but also remember that when others also love what you do, you have the support you need to carry on.

Find those people who love what you do and you will create something amazing in this world. Good luck!

ACKNOWLEDGEMENTS

Just as starting a community is not just the work of a single person, this book was the product of many supportive and generous people. So many people contributed along the way from the Enterprise Sales Forum community to friends I met while at Stack Overflow and DEVBIZOPS to the path of translating that experience into the book you are reading.

In no particular order, I want to acknowledge the generosity and support of the following awesome people!

Sincere thanks and gratitude (and apologies for my sometimes overbearing and compulsive nature) to the many awesome folks that were chapter leaders and volunteers for the Enterprise Sales Forum over the years because without you, none of this would be possible:

Brian Smith, Morgan Ingram, Tyler Bliss, Amanda Bagley, Mike LaTella, Todd Scarborough, Tudor Saitoc, Alex Newman, Alex Siegler, Amanda Brightwell, Brandon Tigges, David Poku, Evan Perkins, Jay Choi, Jo Hester, Jodi Beaubien, Jon Driscoll, Kenny Madden, Kristi Morris, Mark Marostica, Paige Drews, Sarah King, Scott Ingram, Tyler Matheny, Vin Outhavong, Glenn Donovan, Matt Walsh, Meg Kopka, Collette King, Jeremy Leveille, Nadia Stoyanova, Kwesi Sakyi-Gyinae, Rachelle Punzalan, Rhea Buenavista, Kurt Johnson, Benn Jackson, Nick Werle, Alexine Mudawar, Alicia Duddy, Chuck Reotutar, David Lobo, Dulce Melendez, Harry Evans, James Christman, Kevin Walsh, Robert Bednarz, Dan Douglass, Robert Brownd, Mary Beth Cockerham, Dawna Newcomb, Sarah Fricke, Henry Hunter, Jeff Englander, Kerianne Gallagher, Kurt Greening, Mica Longanecker, Nick Boustead, Richard Rothstein, Samantha Alspaugh, Chad Burmeister, Cliff Unger, Kelli Ward, Ryan Donohue, Katie

Williamson, Liz Lally, Nikayla Ratz, Walt Pape, John LaRose, Nick Wei, Olivia Bodnar, David Schlosberg, Alex Berry, Donal McLaughlin, Eleanor Sims, Harry Maxwell, Louise Burgess, Chris Martin, Elaine Tyler, Timothy Antos, Vasile Granaci, Jipei Zhang, Neil Golub, Grace Kim, Brandon Gracey, Fred Ramstedt, Joe Bisagna, Sarah Clarke, Nicole Ward-Taylor, Manoj Rajwani, Nolan Cella, Arthur Shalagin, Aurelio Sisto, Jennifer Low, Nick Pulitano, Tom Livingston, Bryan Elsesser, Meg Hewitt, Doron Greenspan, Jay Theobald, Joshua Hanif, Kyle Poretto, Brandon Frankel, Caitlyn Custer, Donna Valente, David Sill, Stephanie Staiano, Vernon Madison, James Hodges, Jo-Anne Jaspan, Dominic Canterbury, Robert Simmons, Dallas Hogensen, Paul Hlatky, TK Kader, Drew Hoffman, Gwen Lamar, Ian Adams , Luciano Scala, Charmain Tan, Reeta Sabnani, Zeena Kuraisha, Max Legros, Mukundan A P, Raymond Tan, Steve Dana, Adir Zimerman, Cindy Gordon, Joanne Modugno, Miriam Auer, Natalie Koay, Shikha Bindra, Abdul Habboub, Ashwathy Krishna Kumar, Eddy Simmalavong, Erin McLachlan, Gurdeep Singh, Malay Upadhyay, Mark Vukman, Nick Kozik, Palvasha Riaz, Parvez Javeed, Radz Mpofu, Scott Howard, Stephanie Papagni, Tim Peters, Vanesa Andrés, Scott Barker, Alanna Bordignon, Alexander Scott, Brendan Shaughnessy, Cameron Jonker, Robby Jones.

And special shout outs to Mike Pierce, who helped me start what was then the Enterprise Sales Meetup; Cee Bunevich, who was an ardent supporter and mentor from day one; and Christopher Perras and Yoram Stone, who both kept the community going when I got too overwhelmed. You are all awesome humans!

I also heartfully thank all of the members, speakers, and sponsors who joined me on this wild Enterprise Sales Forum ride over the past six years.

Thank you so much to Xiaoyin Qu of Run The World for not only creating an awesome platform for virtual events, but in also helping to support the Enterprise Sales Forum.

My team at Amazon Web Services (AWS) that leads Startup Advocacy, Mackenzie Kosut and Rob DeFeo. As much as I have shared about my experience, they opened my eyes to the scale and opportunities that companies can avail themselves of when they make community building a serious pillar of their customer experience.

Working at Stack Overflow was an invaluable place to learn about online communities and it informed many of the ideas I rolled into the Enterprise Sales Forum and this book. In particular, I wanted to thank Michele Keiper, who taught me so much about building internal communities; Alex Miller who patiently explained the history and guts behind how Stack Overflow works; and the folks on the Community Management team, especially Josh Heyer (AKA shog9), Jon Ericson, and Robert Cartaino, who taught me so much about how online community works at scale.

As a co-organizer for DevOpsDays NYC, it was amazing to see an all-volunteer organization operate at scale firsthand. I want to thank my fellow NYC team members for making it a memorable experience and teaching so much along the process in putting on a world-class event for technical folks: Aaron Aldrich, Adarsh Shah, Ceren Ercen, Matt Kuritz, Priyanka Rao, Russell Kaehler, Jay Gordon, Jerome Moore, Liz Fong-Jones, Matt Titmus, Stefana Mueller, Stephen Thomas, Sumit Agarwal.

Well before I started thinking about community, I got involved with a few folks in NYC that were building a collective space for the city's best entrepreneurs. That turned into WeWork Labs and it exposed me to many awesome people and how powerful a community can be. Thanks to Matt Shampine and Jesse Middleton for inviting me to be part of that journey.

Sincere thanks to the reviewers that so willingly read through very rough drafts and gave their candid feedback to make this a much more valuable resource for readers: Aditya Sahay, Bart Mroz, Catherine DeMartino, Ernest Teh, Hondy Hung, Isha Tripathi, Jeff Szczepanski, Jerome Walter, Joshua Au, Karthik Ragubathy, Mac Reddin, Monica Cellio, Nilesh Gule, Peter Varhol, Ritesh Mehrotra, Shaun Norris, Stephen Dewar, Xin Yi Yap, Brannon McAllister, Rose Barrett, Matt Walsh, Justin Finkelstein, Michael Isvy, Rashmi Nambiar, Divya Gehlot Mishra, Andres Bilbao, Chivas Nambiar, Ozgur Guler, Josh Viney, Jonathan Sroka, José A. Ferreira Queimada, Giuseppe Candela, Deepak Pande, Ravi Rao, Andrew Hyde, and Xiaoyin Qu.

I also owe a debt of gratitude to Nelson Chan, who not only reviewed a draft of this book and wisely suggested some very sound edits, but also helped lead me to my present role at AWS.

There were also many supportive souls over the past year that helped in so many ways just through their kindness and encouragement. Thanks to the Quod AI team, such an awesome startup and founding team in Herve Roussel and Misha Filippov. Thank you to everyone in my Challenge Network for pushing me to raise the bar in my work while still being supportive.

And especially thanks to my sister Danielle, who would always help out in a pinch whether it was with the Enterprise Sales Forum or patiently listening to my insane entrepreneurial musings.

Most of all, my love to my dearest wife and kids, who were patient with me when I was stuck in the dining room writing and editing and cursing for days on end. You are the joy, hope, and treasures of my life!

APPENDIX

WHAT ARE SOME COMMON EMAIL MERGE TECHNOLOGIES?

When sending emails to your community as discussed in the "Promoting Community" chapter, there are a few options of technologies to use:

- ☐ Consumer email marketing tools
- ☐ Mail merge plug-ins with your personal email account
- ☐ Advanced sales prospecting email tools

Any of these options are viable and provide certain advantages and drawbacks. Below are more detailed explanations of each method.

Consumer Email Marketing Tools

These include Constant Contact, Mailchimp, and over a hundred other options, all of which are low-cost or free to use based on the number of subscribers. The advantage of these tools is you can store all of your contacts, have people add themselves through a link to a subscribe form, and create really slick looking emails. The downside is your email will automatically be tagged as a marketing email and low priority. The reason is the sent email identifier is not you, but the identifier of the email provider. If enough people are opening your email though, it may not be a big issue, but be aware that a good portion of your members may never see your emails.

Mail Merge with Personal Email

Both Microsoft Outlook and Google Gmail have options for using mail merge. These are fairly easy to use and below are instructions for each email provider to set this up:

- **Using Outlook for Mail Merge**
- **Using Gmail for Mail Merge**

The key advantage is you are using your own email address, so you can be assured the people you send emails to will have a higher likelihood of seeing your messages. However, your template customization options are limited, which is a bit of a "hackish" approach, as there is no elegant way of handling your contacts and community members, or of adding subscribers.

Advanced Sales Email Tools

The difference with sales email tools is they are meant for outbound sales prospecting, so they are barebones when it comes to formatting, but are powerful when it comes to setting up workflows for scheduling a series of emails, managing and tracking communications, and organizing contacts. The other advantage is you are also using your personal email address to ensure higher deliverability of your emails. The downside is that these tools can be very complex and expensive on a monthly basis compared with the email marketing tools. On the basic end, there are options such as Yesware and HubSpot. On the more complex end, there is Outreach and Salesloft that are geared towards sales prospecting teams and offer more complex functionality. Some useful mid-range options that balance features and cost include Prospect.io and Reply.io.

DO I NEED A CRM SYSTEM?

No. Keep things simple and store your contacts in a spreadsheet. Initially, the only information that matters is Name, Company, Job Title, and Email. If you want to get fancy, you can use a contact management tool like Contacts+ that automatically attaches social network information for your contacts. Once you have a large enough member base and you are past one thousand community members, it may make sense to invest in a low-cost SMB-oriented CRM system. The Enterprise Sales Forum uses is HubSpot, which is free and comes with pre-built integration to Mailchimp,

Eventbrite, and other common SaaS applications.

HOW DO I CHECK-IN ATTENDEES?

As an organizer, you can download the full list of attendees from the Eventbrite, Meetup.com, or whatever service you decide to use for event pages. You can then print out the list or simply check-in attendees on a spreadsheet, directly via the website of the service you are using, or through a mobile check-in app sometimes provided by these services.

The other option is to use a dedicated check-in app. These apps allow you to upload a guest list and to check-in attendees from a browser, tablet, or smartphone. You can also add walk-in guests as well and electronically capture name, email, and payments. The downside is this system needs to be linked to your event/ ticketing service so this process is coordinated and synchronized.

WHAT TOOLS DO I NEED FOR VIRTUAL EVENTS?

This is a fast changing space given the sudden interest in technologies that can help host virtual events and support online community building. Most of the platforms in recent years were oriented around webinars, which can certainly work even though they provide very little in the way of interactivity and viewer engagement.

More modern tools have started to incorporate high-quality video conferencing, greater reliability, and more viewer engagement features. Zoom has been far and away the most successful company in this respect. Despite some security flaws and undesirable features being exploited, the platform has been the most reliably consistent.

Many of the modern conferencing platforms have many of the same key features. They all allow recording of content. They can enable online breakout rooms for smaller groups in a larger event and can accommodate a few hundred attendees. There are interactive features such as polls and Q&A. You can monetize directly through integrating payments and ensure a safe and secure online experience.

The next evolution in conferencing software builds both on scale and in delivering more engaging networking experience. There are large in-person events that have had to go all online. To fulfill this need, startups like Run The World have been able to replicate some of the aspects of in-person events in a virtual setting with multiple breakout rooms, interactive features, and specific networking functionality. For bigger events and companies, data can be collected on attendee interactivity and movement between rooms, then displayed in dashboards to measure what is driving the most engagement.

The Enterprise Sales Forum uses both Zoom and Run The World for online events and have had positive experiences. Both also have reasonable pricing for basic offerings that can fit in the budget of a young community. Plus, there are many others using these platforms and writing about the experiences, so there are people you can reach out to for advice.

Note that many of the most promising technology providers are early stage startups rather than the established technology companies. Changes will come unexpectedly, so expect feature and reliability glitches that impact the experience for attendees. This space is rapidly evolving however, and I expect to see massive innovation in both reliability and features over the next few years. The best advice is before deciding on a platform, search around and chat with other community organizers about what tools they are getting excited about.

WHAT TOOLS & SYSTEMS DOES ENTERPRISE SALES FORUM USE?

There are several different technologies used to run the community, many of which are shared with the General Managers that lead the various global chapters. The following tools used include:

- **Email** – Personalized esfsales.com email account (using Gmail)
- **Google Drive** – Stores all of documents and photos
- **Livestream** – Used to stream events live to the community
- **YouTube** – Hosts the video content
- **Eventbrite** – Manages ticketing and payments, provides an alternative event page

- **Mailchimp** – Platform for the newsletters, event reminders, and member sign-ups
- **Buffer** – Social media scheduling platform to automate social media postings
- **HubSpot** – CRM for managing member data and sponsor opportunities
- **Run The World** – Online events platform for networking and talks
- **Zoom** – Platform for internal team meetings and some online events
- **Amazon Web Services** – Platform that runs the custom website
- **QuickBooks** – Accounting and billing platform
- **Expensify** – Capture receipts and manage expenses
- **Stripe** – Payments processor for credit cards
- **Slack** – Team messaging platform
- **Trello** – Manage workflow for organizing team
- **GIMP** - To create and edit images such as event banners
- **Transferwise** – To send expense reimbursements to chapters

WHAT SOFTWARE DO YOU RECOMMEND TO MANAGE FINANCES?

There are three main applications you will need, but first you need to set up a bank account. If you are using a personal account, it is a good idea to create a separate account just for your community transactions so it is easier to track and then extract when it comes time for taxes. If you have set up a legal entity for the community, then you can register a new account under the name of the entity. In either personal or business banking, you can then use the bank's online software and mobile apps to monitor the account.

For software in the beginning, you will need:

- **Accounting package**
- **Expense tracking**
- **Credit card processing**

For accounting purposes, most software works the same. You can tie it to a bank account and credit cards, and then the software tracks transactions. Most software these days also handle billing, payments, and invoicing. The Enterprise Sales Forum uses QuickBooks, but Wave and Xero are credible options, with Wave being mostly free to use for core services.

Next you will need to track expenses. Not everything may end up being tracked through bank account records, so this allows you to capture those transactions, such as when using cash. More importantly though, the receipts will be needed for taxes purposes, and an app can also help categorize those expenses such as business services, equipment purchases, travel, or food and beverage. Using Expensify for this purpose is recommended.

Lastly, you will need a means to process credit card transactions. Whether for ticketing purposes at events or for billing sponsors, being able to capture credit cards is essential. The best option in my experience is Stripe and a number of other services use Stripe as well. Square has also worked well for on-site event purchases. Note that most ticketing and event platforms will be able to accept credit card payments, so this may not be essential early on for your community.

WHAT SOCIAL MEDIA SITES DO YOU USE?

It is important to use social media effectively and pick the channels that you will regularly use. There is no point to using social media if you will not engage with others and post a constant flow of content to share. The biggest mistake community organizers make is setting up a lot of social media accounts, then getting overwhelmed and not using any of them effectively. Do not create "dead" social media communities!

You can find the Enterprise Sales Forum online properties at the following locations:

- Website: http://enterprisesalesforum.com/
- Twitter: https://twitter.com/Enterprise_Sale
- Facebook Page: https://www.facebook.com/enterprisesales
- LinkedIn Company: https://www.linkedin.com/company/enterprisesalesforum

- ▢ LinkedIn Group: https://www.linkedin.com/groups/8515934
- ▢ Livestream: https://livestream.com/enterprisesales
- ▢ YouTube: http://entsale.co/entsalesvideos

Note that these are a lot of sites to maintain, all of which need to be updated regularly. In whatever the team does, the goal is to ensure each social presence created is as vibrant a part of the community as the in-person events. That takes time and people to keep fresh, engaging, and valuable for members.

As you get started, pick one social media site, and optimize for engagement there. Once you have built up a decent sized audience, branch out by adding one more social media site. You can then use various social media management tools to help distribute content across all your social sites on a regular basis. Options such as Buffer, HootSuite, and Sprout Social are some of the more popular tools, but explore further, as there are plenty of great choices out there, some of which are completely free.

DO I NEED TO BUILD A WEBSITE?

It depends. If you are building an online community not centered around events, then it might make sense. For example, a discussion forum or Q&A knowledge community. That being said, there are plenty of online communities that live purely on Slack, Facebook, Whatsapp, or other existing applications and websites.

The same applies to event-driven communities. You probably do not need a website at first. You want to be experimental and focused on how you invest your time and effort. A website could be a distraction because that leads to many other decisions like logos, color schemes, design, copy, and the platform itself to build, host, and maintain the site. This is too much overhead at the beginning when other things matter more for your launch.

Most event driven communities can initially live on your chosen event platform. Meetup.com, Eventbrite, Run The World, etc., are all suitable places to exist online before investing in a separate website. The benefit is that administration is easier, your data on events and signups is in one place, and it is low maintenance.

One other thing you want to do is have a place to send people that can sign up to your email list. If you use an email marketing platform, many have free tiers and provide a mechanism for building a basic landing page for people to share their details and sign up for upcoming events. The benefit of this approach is it is fast, free, and builds up your email list, which is a critical activity for promoting and growing your community.

If you really insist on having a website, consider waiting for a few events. This way you have a better sense of how the community is coming along and have some media to make the website feel more real. There are plenty of low cost, no code involved web building options these days from the basics like Google Sites and Carrd to more fully featured such as WordPress and Wix.

DO I NEED A DOMAIN NAME?

While a website is not necessary early on, buying a domain name is recommended. Having a domain for your community will allow you to set up a business email account and lock in a name when you are ready to set up your website.

A domain name can be the literal name of your community or some close variation such as an abbreviated name. For example, the Enterprise Sales Forum uses both types of domain names. The website uses the literal name enterprisesalesforum.com, while email uses the abbreviated esfsales.com so that email addresses are shorter to type.

DO I NEED AN EMAIL ADDRESS FOR THE COMMUNITY?

Yes, using your personal email address might suffice during your launch. However, soon after you will want to switch to a non-personal email account that can be used by the community organizing team.

The reason for a separate account is it makes coordination easier. All correspondence is in one place, thus putting all sign-ups for services the community uses into a centrally accessible group account. The other advantage is it does not expose anyone's personal email address.

Opt for a low cost paid account with Microsoft Office 365 or Google G Suite, which comes with email, office tools like word processing and spreadsheets, and sufficient storage for video and photo files. There are also many other lower cost options, such as Zoho Workplace, that might better suit your needs and budget.

DO WE NEED A CODE OF CONDUCT?

There has been a growing trend in the past few years for events to have guidelines that explicitly call out unprofessional behavior and the consequences for such behavior. The goal is to clarify what behaviors and language are unacceptable so all event participants can expect a safe and respectful event experience free from harassment in any form.

I recommend crafting your own Code of Conduct (CoC) at some point early on in your community's development. Every major conference now has a CoC and many communities have also created their own CoCs. Whether you feel it should be something you do from the very beginning or later on depends on many factors. At a minimum, it is recommended to incorporate early on a statement supporting respect for diversity and inclusion as a core community value and making it explicit that harassment will not be tolerated.

When you are ready to craft your formal CoC, you can go to this site for ideas and examples on structure and recommended language. Take note that it is important to craft a document you can enforce, otherwise it does not have any value. Therefore, never blindly copy another community's documents; create a CoC that reflects the values and culture of your community.

The last step in formalizing your CoC is to allow the community to freely comment on the language. This both engenders trust that this is a community-oriented effort and demonstrates transparency. Once the community agrees the CoC truly represents its interests, there should be no questions or push back if an occasion arises in which enforcement action is necessary.

Remember, the CoC is just one component in supporting a more welcoming and inclusive experience for all community members. By regularly supporting content, speakers, promotion, sponsorships, and day-of-event management that demonstrates welcome and inclusion, you create a safe environment for all members, volunteers, speakers, and staff.

DO WE NEED TO REGISTER A COMPANY?

It depends. It is important to observe local laws, national laws, and business regulations, as it pertains to your community, and seek the advice of a licensed legal professional. While many communities operate without formal registration, that may not be relevant to your community based on size, revenue, etc.

Outside of the legal question, registering your community as an organization may have certain benefits, despite the added burdens. Some venue hosts and sponsors, for example, might require signing a contract that explicitly outlines liabilities and indemnification before agreeing to provide space or sponsorship. Some venues may ask for a minimum amount of insurance coverage as well. In these cases, creating a legal entity may be beneficial as you scale your community.

The biggest benefit of registering the community is it creates a clear separation between organizers and your community, thus protecting organizers from personal liability in the event of legal proceedings against the community. This is known as "corporate shield" and applies as long as the organization complies with certain expectations of a legal entity in good standing. In other words, be transparent, keep good records, and adhere to business regulations.

Ultimately, the question of whether you should register is one you will need to make based on your circumstances. Once your community reaches a certain scale, it may be an evitable next step.

HOW DO I BUILD A LAUNCH ORGANIZING LIST?

The best strategy to building the list of people you think could play some part in your community is to keep it simple. This is not a comprehensive contact database building and cleanup effort, but a way to keep track of who you want to be involved in your nascent community and how those people would participate.

An easy way to start is to build the list from people you already know. Those contacts might be in a contact management app or email client like Google Contacts or Microsoft Outlook. You might have a customer relationship management system like Salesforce, HubSpot, or Pipedrive where you store contacts.

The next obvious place to check for contacts is LinkedIn. Based on the audience, there may be better sites, such as GitHub for developers or Dribbble for designers, but most professions are well-represented on LinkedIn at this point. Focusing on LinkedIn, however, you can go into settings and request a download of all your 1st degree connections.

The downloaded list will include the following columns: Name, Company, Position, Email, and Connected On. This is good enough to start, though be aware that LinkedIn stopped providing email addresses of your connections unless a contact opts-in to having emails included in these data downloads.

Email is an important data point to collect for your launch list. Nothing works as well as email for communicating widely to a lot of people at once. Email will be your primary channel to reach out for help and to drum up interest in the community.

You could manually collect emails from each LinkedIn contact, but that is very time consuming. There are a number of tools available now to collect emails from your contacts automatically for a reasonable fee that can do the work for you in hours, instead of days. While tools will come and go, there are three worth mentioning: SalesQL, Skrapp, and Snov. Each tool can gather email addresses from LinkedIn contacts, plus they have the added value of collecting other information, such as location and industry, if that is important for your list.

When you have collected the emails addresses, you can begin to build out the spreadsheet. In addition to information such as Name, Company, Position, and Email, you want to add a field to categorize your contacts called Category. This field is used to identify how each contact could be involved in the community. For example, a contact could be a potential MEMBER, LEADER, VOLUNTEER, INFLUENCER, SPEAKER, SPONSOR, or NOT RELEVANT. All contacts would be part of your outreach email list, with the exception of those tagged NOT RELEVANT.

DO YOU HAVE AN EXAMPLE OF A LAUNCH PACKET?

Yes, included below is the template created for use by chapter organizers in the Enterprise Sales Forum. This is much longer than what would normally be sent to people you want to help promote your community and launch event, since the template is meant to address different situations and stages of community growth.

Feel free to use this template and/or customize it. The idea is to choose and customize the sections so it is concise, relevant, and easy for people receiving this document to take action. In some cases, it may be preferable to just send a short blurb and one or two links to share over social media. Remember, the less effort you require of people to help, the greater the chance those people will respond and follow through on helping.

Enterprise Sales Forum – Launch Document

Thank you for your help in spreading the word about the Enterprise Sales Forum as we get ready to host our first event! In this document there is information about the community, specifics on the upcoming event, and quick ways you can share and help us as we prepare to launch the community.

ABOUT ENTERPRISE SALES FORUM

The Enterprise Sales Forum is a community for B2B sales professionals and leaders to share ideas, network with peers, and learn from each other. Our vision is that sales is a profession, anyone can learn to excel at sales, and sales is highly collaborative. Our community provides the resources to help motivated individuals strive for professional excellence and achievement in sales. We offer quality content and discussions through regularly scheduled in-person or virtual events that offer practical applications and interesting perspectives without overt commercial influence.

LAUNCH EVENT DETAILS

We plan to start a community in [CITY] by creating a launch event to drive awareness and begin to build the membership of the community.

EVENT DESCRIPTION

For our initial event on [DATE] we have invited [SPEAKER] of [COMPANY] to speak on the topic [TOPIC]. [DESCRIPTION OF TALK]. [WHAT ATTENDEES SHOULD EXPECT].

VENUE & DATE

- **[VENUE]**, [ADDRESS] ([MAP_LINK])
- **[DATE] at [TIME]**

AGENDA

- **Check-in / Networking**   6:00 PM – 7:00 PM
- **Talk w/ [SPEAKER(S)]**   7:00 PM – 7:45 PM
- **Audience Q & A**   7:00 PM – 8:00 PM
- **Closing / Networking**   8:00 PM – 8:30 PM

AUDIENCE

We are targeting 75-100 people in the audience for our initial event. Our audience consists of sales leaders & managers ranging from startups to large companies. We also attract a large contingent of tech startup founders looking to learn more about enterprise sales and leadership practices.

EVENT SIGNUP

The main link to sign up for the event: **[EVENT PAGE LINK]**

HOW TO SHARE

SOCIAL MEDIA

You can find the Enterprise Sales Forum on the Web and at the following social media sites:

- Twitter: [TWITTER_LINK]
- Facebook: [FACEBOOK_LINK]
- LinkedIn: [LINKEDIN_LINK]
- YouTube: [YOUTUBE_LINK]
- Livestream: [LIVESTREAM_LINK]
- Instagram: [INSTAGRAM_LINK]

SOCIAL SHARING

Our Twitter account is **@Enterprise_Sale** and community hashtag is **#ESFSALES**. Use the following **[TWEET_LINK]** or **[LINKEDIN_UPDATE]** to share across your professional network. Feel free to modify.

> *Join me for the launch of the [CITY] Enterprise Sales Forum w/ [TWITTER_HANDLE] on [TOPIC]! [SIGN_UP_LINK] #ESFSALES*

EVENT BANNER

[PLACE_IMAGE_HERE]

Link to banner: **[BANNER IMAGE LINK]**

EMAIL SHARING

Short "what" version:

The [CITY] Enterprise Sales Forum is a community for B2B sales professionals to network, share innovative ideas in sales, and learn from successful sales leaders. The inaugural event is [DATE] at [VENUE] and you can sign up at: **[SIGNUP_LINK]**

Longer "why" version:

Mark Birch, an entrepreneur and confirmed sales geek, saw that B2B companies struggled mightily with building and supporting enterprise sales. He launched the Enterprise Sales Forum to bring sales professionals and leaders to network at monthly events that feature engaging speakers and content focused on innovations in enterprise sales methods. I encourage you to sign up for their inaugural event [DATE] with [SPEAKER(S)], on [TOPIC]: **[SIGNUP_LINK]**

SPONSORSHIP

Sponsorships are a means for us to host high quality events and help us to grow our community. Some sponsors we work with include [SPONSORS] that are committed to building up strong sales communities.

If you have questions about becoming a sponsor for the community, please contact [NAME] at [EMAIL] to discuss the details on different programs and costs available to sponsors.

QUESTIONS

You may contact [NAME], the founder, at [PHONE_NUMBER] or [EMAIL] if you have questions about how best to share our community or anything else related to our launch.

DO YOU HAVE A SAMPLE CHECKLIST I CAN USE?

Yes, included below are two checklists. The first is the Day of Event Management Checklist to manage the day of tasks in running an event as well as some critical before and after event tasks the person in charge of event management should track. The second is the Event Organizer's Planning Checklist, a longer checklist for all the tasks that go into organizing an event over the course of many weeks. Feel free to modify these as you see fit for your purposes.

Day of Event Management Checklist – Enterprise Sales Forum

Day Before Event

- ☐ Confirm Catering and Production Requirements with Venue Host
- ☐ Confirm roles with LOCAL ESF TEAM MEMBERS to support event
- ☐ Confirm arrival time and venue location with speakers
- ☐ Confirm attendance by sponsors (they receive free sponsor tickets)
- ☐ Create Event Presentation using **EVENT PRESENTATION TEMPLATE** in each Chapter Folder with the title form TEMPLATE-[CITY_CODE]_ESF_BANNER+DECK.pptx
  - ☐ **SAMPLE TEMPLATE** found in 00_TEMPLATE folder

Day of Event

- ☐ Check weather, determine whether weather conditions warrant canceling event
- ☐ Publish Livestream page using **LIVESTEAM SETUP** guide and share over social media
- ☐ Bring the following items
  - ☐ iPads
  - ☐ Tripod
  - ☐ Name tags
  - ☐ Markers
  - ☐ Laptop with power cable
  - ☐ Cables to connect laptop to projector (HDMI adapters, etc.)
  - ☐ Camera (optional)
- ☐ Download and send Guest List Report to Venue Host by 12 PM
- ☐ Arrive at least ONE HOUR before start time of event
- ☐ Check Wi-Fi access requirements
- ☐ Check Bathroom access and get keycards/codes if required
- ☐ Check Security / Building Access is coordinated and people can enter venue
- ☐ Setup iPads with check-in software
- ☐ Setup check-in desk with iPads, name tags, and markers
- ☐ Setup phone for Livestream; ensure connectivity and correct event is selected (DO NOT START)
- ☐ Setup A/V equipment

- ☐ Sound system on and mics checked for volume and feedback
- ☐ Projector on, connected to laptop, and showing Event Presentation
- ☐ Lighting is set up (if necessary)
- ☐ Setup food & beverage with cups, plates, utensils & napkins and provide labels for food
- ☐ Ensure there are adequate trash / recycle bins in the area of the event
- ☐ Setup chairs for attendees
- ☐ Setup chairs / presenting area for speakers & moderator
- ☐ Spend 15 minutes with speakers & moderator over drinks to prep for talk

MC Event Announcements

RIGHT BEFORE TALK BEGINS

- ☐ Check with AV Manager that Livestream started and broadcasting (check both sound & video)
- ☐ Announce two minutes before talk begins to invite attendees to find their seats
- ☐ Thank everyone for attending
- ☐ Encourage sharing on social media using #[CITY_CODE]Sales on Twitter @Enterprise_Sale and on Instagram using #salesmeetup tag
- ☐ Share preamble on the why and what and origins of ESF
- ☐ Thank venue host for welcoming our community into their offices
- ☐ Thank sponsors and invite to share 1 minute pitch if in attendance
- ☐ Open up community announcements time - anything on hiring, promotions, good news
- ☐ Thank speakers and moderator
- ☐ Ask for a round of applause

AFTER TALK CONCLUDES

- ☐ Thank speakers and moderator
- ☐ Ask for a round of applause
- ☐ Thank sponsors again

☐ Thank venue host again

☐ Announce next event topic, date & location

☐ Announce location of afterparty

☐ Thank everyone for attending and wish them a good evening

Post Event

☐ Stop Livestream recording, post to site, and breakdown camera and tripod

☐ Turn off projector and collect laptop and projector cables

☐ Collect iPads, name tags, and markers from check-in area

☐ Return mics to venue host

☐ DEPENDING ON ARRANGEMENT WITH VENUE HOST:

  ☐ Turn off sound system

  ☐ Clean up food & beverage items

  ☐ Breakdown seats and speaker area

  ☐ Turn off lights and ensure facility locked

Day After Event

☐ Download Attendees Report from Ticket System and upload to **ESF DROPBOX FOLDER**

☐ Upload photos from event to **ESF DROPBOX FOLDER**

☐ Send Thank You Email to Local Sponsors, Speakers, Local ESF Team

☐ Send to Recap Event Announcement Email in **MEMBER COMMUNICATIONS TEMPLATE**

Event Organizers Planning Checklist – Enterprise Sales Forum

Event Planning

COMPLETED **AT LEAST 3 MONTHS BEFORE** HOSTING EVENT

☐ Add Event Information to **EVENT SCHEDULE** spreadsheet

- ☐ Date/Day/Time
- ☐ Title
- ☐ Venue/Location - name of venue and address
- ☐ Format (PRESENTATION, PANEL, FIRESIDE CHAT, WORKSHOP, ROUNDTABLE, OTHER)
- ☐ Description - two to three sentences max
- ☐ Event Page Link
- ☐ Speaker(s)
- ☐ Food & Beverage (Y/N)
- ☐ Collect Speaker Information on **SPEAKERS TAB** in **CITY EVENT PLANNING DATABASE**
  - ☐ Name
  - ☐ Company
  - ☐ Job Title
  - ☐ LinkedIn URL
  - ☐ Twitter Profile URL
  - ☐ Email (Work) and/or Email (Personal)
  - ☐ Phone (Mobile) and/or Phone (Work)
  - ☐ Topic Ideas
  - ☐ Meetup Date scheduled
  - ☐ Short Bio - three to five sentences max
  - ☐ Headshot - high-res color profile photo
  - ☐ Company Website
- ☐ Create Event Page using Ticketing System
  - ☐ Use **EVENT PAGE TEMPLATE** if not editing a previous Event Page
  - ☐ Check topic, speakers, date, and venue match **EVENT SCHEDULE**
- ☐ Create Event Banner using **EVENT BANNER TEMPLATE** in each Chapter Folder, referring to **CREATE BANNERS USING POWERPOINT** (watch **instructional video**)
  - ☐ Ensure pixel dimensions are 640 x 360
  - ☐ Triple check spelling
  - ☐ Check topic, speakers, date, and venue match **EVENT SCHEDULE**
- ☐ Add Event to Livestream using **LIVESTEAM SETUP** guide
  - ☐ DO NOT publish event yet

4 Weeks Out from Event

☐ Complete and send Speaker Packet to speakers using **SPEAKER PACKET TEMPLATE**

☐ Confirm DATE, VENUE with VENUE HOST and send Speaker Packet to them

☐ Confirm availability of LOCAL ESF TEAM MEMBERS to attend and support event

    ☐ Moderator

    ☐ MC

    ☐ Event Manager

    ☐ Social Media Manager

    ☐ A/V Manager (presentation, video, photos)

    ☐ Welcome Team

☐ Send 1st Event Announcement Email in **MEMBER COMMUNICATIONS TEMPLATE**

    ☐ Focus on event announcement

☐ Send Promotion Reminder Email to Local Sponsors, Speakers, Local ESF Team, HQ ESF Team

3 Weeks Out from Event

☐ Send 2nd Event Announcement Email in **MEMBER COMMUNICATIONS TEMPLATE**

    ☐ Focus on content for event

☐ Send Promotion Reminder Email to Local Sponsors, Speakers, Local ESF Team, HQ ESF Team

☐ Venue Host Confirmation Call

    ☐ Confirm dates and space

    ☐ Confirm production requirements in **EVENT SPECIFICATIONS GUIDE**

    ☐ Confirm accessibility requirements in **ACCESSIBILITY CHECKLIST**

2 Weeks Out from Event

☐ Send 3rd Event Announcement Email in **MEMBER COMMUNICATIONS TEMPLATE**

☐ Focus on speaker(s) for event
☐ Send Promotion Reminder Email to Local Sponsors, Speakers, Local ESF Team, HQ ESF Team
☐ Check registrations and if low, consult with HQ ESF Team
☐ Speaker Confirmation Call
    ☐ Confirm availability and production requirements including A/V support
    ☐ Review topic, format, and speaker questions

1 Week Out from Event

☐ Send 4th Event Announcement Email in **MEMBER COMMUNICATIONS TEMPLATE**
    ☐ Focus on sharing event and inviting a friend
☐ Send Promotion Reminder Email to Local Sponsors, Speakers, Local ESF Team, HQ ESF Team
☐ Check registrations and if low, consult with HQ ESF Team
☐ Publish Livestream page using **LIVESTEAM SETUP** guide and share over social media

Day Before Event

☐ Confirm Catering and Production Requirements with Venue Host
☐ Confirm roles with LOCAL ESF TEAM MEMBERS to support event
☐ Confirm arrival time and venue location with speakers
☐ Confirm attendance by sponsors (they receive free sponsor tickets)
☐ Create Event Presentation using **EVENT PRESENTATION TEMPLATE** in each Chapter Folder with the title form TEMPLATE-[CITY_CODE]_ESF_BANNER+DECK.pptx
    ☐ **SAMPLE TEMPLATE** found in 00_TEMPLATE folder

Day of Event

☐ Check weather, determine whether weather conditions warrant canceling event
☐ Bring the following items

- [ ] iPads
- [ ] Tripod
- [ ] Name tags
- [ ] Markers
- [ ] Laptop with power cable
- [ ] Cables to connect laptop to projector (HDMI adapters, etc.)
- [ ] Camera (optional)
- [ ] Download and send Guest List Report to Venue Host by 12 PM
- [ ] Arrive at least ONE HOUR before start time of event
- [ ] Check Wi-Fi access requirements
- [ ] Check Bathroom access and get keycards/codes if required
- [ ] Check Security / Building Access is coordinated and people can enter venue
- [ ] Setup iPads with check-in software
- [ ] Setup check-in desk with iPads, name tags and markers
- [ ] Setup phone for Livestream, ensure connectivity and correct event is selected (DO NOT START)
- [ ] Setup A/V equipment
  - [ ] Sound system on and mics checked for volume and feedback
  - [ ] Projector on, connected to laptop, and showing Event Presentation
  - [ ] Lighting is setup (if necessary)
- [ ] Setup food & beverage with cups, plates, utensils & napkins and provide labels for food
- [ ] Ensure there are adequate trash / recycle bins in the area of the event
- [ ] Setup chairs for attendees
- [ ] Setup chairs / presenting area for speakers & moderator
- [ ] Spend 15 minutes with speakers & moderator over drinks to prep for talk

MC Event Announcements

RIGHT BEFORE TALK BEGINS

- [ ] Check with AV Manager that Livestream started and broadcasting (check both sound & video)

- ☐ Announce two minutes before talk begins to invite attendees to find their seats
- ☐ Thank everyone for attending
- ☐ Encourage sharing on social media using #[CITY_CODE]Sales on Twitter @Enterprise_Sale and on Instagram using #salesmeetup tag
- ☐ Share preamble on the why and what and origins of ESF
- ☐ Thank venue host for welcoming our community into their offices
- ☐ Thank sponsors and invite to share 1 minute pitch if in attendance
- ☐ Open up community announcements time - anything on hiring, promotions, good news
- ☐ Thank speakers and moderator
- ☐ Ask for a round of applause

AFTER TALK CONCLUDES

- ☐ Thank speakers and moderator
- ☐ Ask for a round of applause
- ☐ Thank sponsors again
- ☐ Thank venue host again
- ☐ Announce next event topic, date & location
- ☐ Announce location of afterparty
- ☐ Thank everyone for attending and wish them a good evening

Post Event

- ☐ Stop Livestream recording, post to site, and breakdown camera and tripod
- ☐ Turn off projector and collect laptop and projector cables
- ☐ Collect iPads, name tags, and markers from check-in area
- ☐ Return mics to venue host
- ☐ DEPENDING ON ARRANGEMENT WITH VENUE HOST:
  - ☐ Turn off sound system
  - ☐ Clean up food & beverage items
  - ☐ Breakdown seats and speaker area
  - ☐ Turn off lights and ensure facility locked

Day After Event

- ☐ Download Attendees Report from Ticketing System and upload to **ESF DROPBOX FOLDER**
- ☐ Upload photos from event to **ESF DROPBOX FOLDER**
- ☐ Send Thank You Email to Local Sponsors, Speakers, Local ESF Team
- ☐ Send to Recap Event Announcement Email in **MEMBER COMMUNICATIONS TEMPLATE**

QUESTIONS

If you want to learn more about community building or have specific questions from reading this guide, feel free to reach out to the author **Mark Birch**, Founder of DEV.BIZ.OPS and Enterprise Sales Forum. He can be reached over social media and he welcomes you to send a personal note to him on **LinkedIn** or **Twitter**.

ABOUT ENTERPRISE SALES FORUM

WHAT WE DO

The <u>Enterprise Sales Forum,</u> from its onset, was created as a community for B2B sales professionals and sales leaders to share ideas, network with peers, and learn from each other. Our community is built on the notion that sales is a profession, anyone can learn to excel at sales, and sales is not a lonely pursuit. Sales takes a team, a community, and a culture to support and inspire individuals striving for professional excellence and achievement.

OUR VALUES

The foundation of our community is built upon these four core values:

- **Being Member-Centric**
- **Excellence in Content**
- **Supportive and Collaborative**
- **Foster Sales Innovation**

Our values guide how we lead the community, from the events we host, to the speakers we invite, to the sponsors with whom we work. We want to ensure members receive the full benefit and value of the time they invest towards participating in our community. Therefore, we strive to offer quality content and discussions that offer practical applications, present new and interesting perspectives, and steers away from overt commercial influence.

ABOUT THE AUTHOR

Mark Birch is a community builder, entrepreneur, business development expert, and startup advisor based in Singapore and NYC.

He currently works at Amazon Web Services (AWS) as a Startup Advocate helping to support the community of startups & entrepreneurs across Asia-Pacific. He is the founder of **DEV.BIZ.OPS**, a newsletter about technology innovation and transformation. He also founded the **Enterprise Sales Forum**, a global community of 25,000 B2B sales professionals that meet in-person and virtually through local chapters to share ideas, network with peers, and learn new skills.

Previously, Mark was at Stack Overflow to help launch their Enterprise SaaS Q&A platform and then led efforts to expand business in APAC. Before that he worked at a diverse group of leading technology companies, including Oracle, E.piphany and Siebel, in sales as an individual contributor and in leadership roles.

Mark graduated with a Bachelor of Science in Electrical Engineering from Boston University. In his non-working hours, he likes to tour around Chinatown exploring dumplings shacks, and he can generally be seen rocking out to extreme metal.

ABOUT THE BOOK

A practical guide for community builders on building and scaling professional communities that thrive and transform the lives of the people within them through virtual and in-person events.

Community is a hot topic in 2020. Enterprises, startups, investors, entrepreneurs, and creators are all jumping on board launching communities or building products for communities. This is especially timely given a global pandemic that has left people longing for human connection.

And then there are the people like Mark Birch who just wanted to bring salespeople together.

When Mark started the Enterprise Sales Forum, he did not have a big vision; it was just his way to convince salespeople and startup founders to meet and help each other. What started in a sweaty conference room for 50 people six years ago eventually blossomed into a community of 25,000 members across 20 cities globally.

Community-in-a-Box is a how-to guide into building and scaling a community from the ground up or reinvigorating existing communities. From the experiences of the Enterprise Sales Forum and other communities he launched, Mark weaves those stories into a book that leads you past the minefields and mistakes so you can confidently launch and grow a healthy community.

Even though we all come to community building with our own motivations, the end result is a labor of love that positively impacts the lives of many. Through this book, you will also feel the impact of the power of community and what it takes to grab the spark and start a movement!